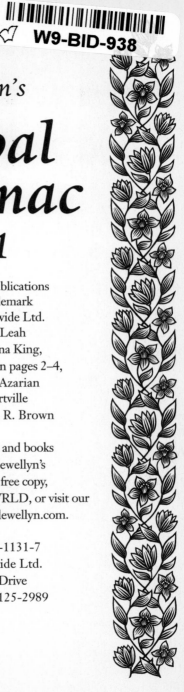

Llewellyn's

Herbal Almanac

2011

© 2010 Llewellyn Publications
is a registered trademark
of Llewellyn Worldwide Ltd.
Editing: Sharon Leah
Interior Art: © Fiona King,
excluding illustrations on pages 2–4,
which are © Mary Azarian
Cover Images: Artville
Cover Design: Kevin R. Brown

You can order annuals and books
from *New Worlds*, Llewellyn's
catalog. To request a free copy,
call toll free: 1-877-NEW WRLD, or visit our
Web site at http://www.llewellyn.com.

ISBN 978-0-7387-1131-7
Llewellyn Worldwide Ltd.
2143 Wooddale Drive
Woodbury, MN 55125-2989

Table of Contents

Growing and Gathering Herbs

Culinary Herbs

Herbs for Health and Beauty

Herb Crafts

Herb History, Myth, and Lore

Moon Signs, Phases, and Tables

Introduction to Llewellyn's Herbal Almanac

The herbal landscape is an ever-evolving one. The slow warming of our planet has seen temperate climates creeping toward the poles, while consumer trends prompt more immediate changes. But through it all, home-grown herbs still make a lasting impact. *Llewellyn's 2011 Herbal Almanac* takes a look at the year-round effects of herbs, re-examining the research on uses of herbs as medicine, as culinary spices, as cosmetics, and more. This year we once again tap into practical, historical, and just plain enjoyable aspects of herbal knowledge—using herbs to help people manage headaches, fibromyalgia, and their libido; to combat pesky insects; to make infusions, tinctures, and teas; and, of course, trying out new recipes. And we bring to these pages some of the most innovative and original thinkers and writers on herbs.

Growing, preparing, and using herbs allows us to focus on the old ways—when men and women around the world knew and understood the power of herbs. Taking a step back to a simpler time is important today as the pace of everyday life quickens and demands more and more of our energy—leaving precious little room for beauty, good food, health, love, and friendship. This state of affairs is perhaps not terribly surprising considering so many of us are out of touch with the beauty, spirituality, and health-giving properties of the natural world. Many of us spend too much of our lives rushing about in a technological bubble. We forget to focus on the parts of life that can bring us back into balance and harmony.

Though it's getting more difficult, you can still find ways to escape the rat race once in a while. People are still striving to make us all more aware of the uplifting, beautiful ways that herbs can affect our lives. In the 2011 edition of the *Herbal Almanac*, the various authors pay tribute to the ideals of beauty and balance in relation to the health-giving and beautifying properties of herbs. Whether it comes in the form of natural herbal baths, crafting your own skin lotion, or a new favorite recipe, herbs can clearly make a positive impact in your life.

Herbs are the perfect complement to the power of the mind, an ancient tool whose time has come back around to help us restore balance in our lives. More and more people are using herbs, growing and gathering them, and studying them for their enlivening and healing properties. We, the editor and authors of this volume, encourage the treatment of the whole organism—of the person and of the planet—with herbal goodness.

Growing and Gathering Herbs

Gather & Preserve Summer Herbs & Flowers

⤜ by Elizabeth Barrette ⤛

Fresh flowers look beautiful, but they never last long. However, you can learn ways of preserving flowers, leaves, seedpods, and other interesting plant parts. Certain varieties boast exceptional ability to retain their color and shape over time, and these make striking displays.

"Everlasting" Species

To grow an effective "everlasting" garden, choose flowers and herbs known for their endurance, rich colors, strong cohesion, sturdy stems, and attractive shapes. They will dry reliably and serve well in many crafts. Here are some species favored by crafters:

Anise Hyssop

The anise hyssop (*Agastache foeniculum*) produces bright red tubular flowers and requires little care to thrive. Dry for use in bouquets or press the individual flowers. Hyssop makes a pleasant ingredient in potpourri or sachets and wreaths.

Baby's Breath

Hang baby's breath (*Gypsophila elegans*) to dry in bunches. The tiny white blossoms are among the most popular "filler" flowers for bouquets and wreaths.

Bachelor's Button

Bachelor's button (*Centaurea cyanus*) is known both for its vivid flowers and its fuzzy silver-gray foliage that make this plant attractive for drying. The blooms range from light blue to violet, but they can also be pink or white. Blossoms can be dried in desiccant to preserve their shape or pressed flat.

Bristly Foxtail

Bristly foxtail (*Setaria verticillata*) comes in green or yellow varieties and is considered a weed, so you may want to wildcraft it instead of growing it. The long seed heads make an attractive accent in bouquets or wreaths.

Bunny-tail Grass

Bunny-tail grass (*Lagurus ovatus*), an easy-to-grow plant, is among the most popular ornamental grasses used by crafters. It forms tufts of leaves topped by thumb-sized seed heads that bob in the wind. The natural cream color of the seed heads takes dye very well. Use the seed heads in bouquets.

Cattail

Cattail (*Typha latifolia*) is a marsh plant that is known for its brown seed heads. The seed heads may be long and thin or short and round. Display cattails in a tall vase.

Chinese Lantern

The perennial Chinese lantern (*Physalis franchetii*) spreads by underground rhizomes, so contain it in a pot or solitary bed. After the white flowers fade, the plant produces a number of inflated papery "lanterns" that change from green to bright orange. Harvest when these reach peak color, leaving them attached to the sturdy stems (remove the shrivelled leaves later). Chinese lanterns add color and visual interest to bouquets.

Cockscomb

Cockscomb (*Celosia argentea*) 'Kimono' cultivars bloom in soft shades of peach, pink, mauve, and yellow. 'Century' cultivars bloom in brilliant shades of pink, red, orange, and yellow. The flowers take many different shapes, including plumes, globes, spires, and the classic wavy "cockscomb" style. They give texture to dried bouquets.

Globe Thistle

Globe thistle (*Echinops ritro*) is a vigorous perennial that is grown for its spiky blue flowers and its blue-green foliage. Flower globes should be dried in desiccant to preserve their shape. Use them in arrangements to add texture.

Globe Amaranth

When dried, the charming globe amaranth (*Gomphrena globosa*) adds color and texture to bouquets or wreaths. Its pom-pom flowers come in shades of red, pink, mauve, lavender, and white.

Honesty

Honesty comes in both annual and perennial forms (*Lunaria annua* is an annual; *Lunaria rediviva* is a perennial). The seeds form in pale, translucent disks that make a striking addition to bouquets. The blue or purple flowers may also be pressed for use in suncatchers.

Larkspur

Larkspur (*Consolida ambigua*) blooms in many shades of blue, purple, pink, and white. They press beautifully for framed arrangements or suncatchers.

Lavender

Some lavender (*Lavandula angustifolia*) cultivars form compact clumps, while others bush out more. All are intensely fragrant, and the flower stalks emerge with sturdy stems and form tufts of blue or lavender flowers at the ends. Cut the stems very close to the ground and dry them in bunches to use in bouquets; you can also weave the stems into fanciful shapes. For potpourri, you can cut off just the flower heads, dry them on screens, then crumble them.

Lotus

The lotus (*Nelumbo nucifera*) is an aquatic perennial that sprouts vigorously from the mud and is native to warm regions. Large round leaves and exquisite peach-colored flowers make it a spectacular sight in ponds. But it's the weird seedpods you want for drying; they make an interesting addition to bouquets. These can be dyed to achieve a variety of colors or spray-painted metallic tones.

Marjoram

A member of the mint family, marjoram (*Origanum vulgare*) has pale green foliage that is intensely aromatic and dries well for use in potpourri or wreaths. The pink flowers may be pressed for framed arrangements or suncatchers.

Northern Sea Oats

The northern sea oats (*Chasmanthium latifolium*) plant sprouts elegant arching stems with pendant seed heads that change color from green to copper to rich brown. These are easy to dry for use in bouquets.

Pansy

Pansy (*Viola wittrockiana*) appears in all colors, with many bicolors or tricolors. Pansies are famous for their little "faces." Press the flowers for use in framed arrangements or suncatchers.

Pompon Dahlia

The perennial pompon dahlia (*Dahlia hortensis*) is often grown as an annual. Its flowers come in white, pink, red, yellow, and flashy bicolors. Use a desiccant to support the fluffy petals while they dry. These flowers add color to arrangements.

Poppy

Poppy (*Papaver spp.*) comes in every hot shade of red, orange, yellow, or pink, as well as pastels and white. The petals rarely hold their bold colors when dried, but you can try pressing them. Crafters grow this plant for its seedpods (different varieties have subtly different shapes of round or oblong pods topped with wrinkled little hats). The seedpods are often dyed or painted for use in bouquets or wreaths.

Queen Anne's Lace

Queen Anne's lace (*Daucus carota*), also known as wild carrot, has lacy leaves on sturdy stems that bear pannicles of tiny white flowers. The heads may be flat or cup-shaped. This plant has many craft uses; its leaves and flowers can be pressed flat for use in framed arrangements or suncatchers, and the flowers can be picked in full bloom and dried flat, or allowed to dry upright on the plant (where they will form cups). Either the leaves or flowers may then be used in bouquets.

Rose

Roses (*Rosa spp.*) come in an extensive range of sizes and colors from red, orange, yellow, pale green, mauve, pink, and white, to lavender-blue and even chocolate. There are many bicolors and a few tricolors, too. Cut roses at the bud stage and dry in desiccant, or cut as flowers open and dry whole in desiccant, or remove the petals and dry them on a screen. Petals may also be pressed. Roses in any form make excellent potpourri.

Buds may be wired onto a wreath or used in bouquets, and pressed petals are pretty in frames or suncatchers.

Scarlet Sage

Scarlet sage (*Salvia coccinea*) blooms in warm shades of scarlet, burgundy, coral, apricot, and off-white. Leaves are usually green, but some cultivars are chocolate-colored. Pick off the flowers and press them for use in framed arrangements or suncatchers.

Statice

Statice (*Limonium sinuatum*) comes in shades of mauve, red, coral, pale yellow, violet, lavender, and white. Blossoms in the purple color range last especially well. Dry the flowers upside down for use in bouquets, or press them flat for framed arrangements and suncatchers.

Strawflower

Strawflowers (*Helichrysum bracteatum*) retain color well and last practically forever. Flower shapes include globes, buttons, puffs, and daisylike figures. Look for pink, red, orange, yellow, purple, maroon, and white blooms. Dry these upside down or in desiccant. They make lovely bouquets and wreaths.

Yarrow

Yarrow (*Achillea millefolium*) comes in many colors, but yellow-colored yarrow retains its beauty the most when dried. Its tiny flowers form large heads. Silica gel gives the best drying results. The delicate feathery leaves may also be pressed for use in framed arrangements or suncatchers.

Gathering and Drying Plants

Pick flowers and plants for drying on a warm sunny day. Flowers may be picked either as buds or close to their prime. They will open more as they dry. Flowers in the pink to orange, or blue to purple, range retain their colors best. Seedpods should be picked slightly green so they do not pop open and lose their seeds. Seek herbs and foliage that have graceful, interesting shapes, and avoid wilted or damaged plants, because the drying process makes defects more conspicuous.

Find a warm, dry place that has good ventilation and not too much direct sunlight, which causes fading. Make sure curious pets or children won't get into your plants while they're drying.

Flowers and seedpods can be air dried, and most plants will dry well when hung upside down in bunches. Use cotton string to bind four to eight stems together and suspend them in a safe place. Some flowers—baby's breath, poppy seed heads, or Chinese lanterns, for example—dry better upright. Place several stems in a large vase, but not too many, because they shouldn't be packed in too tight. Top-heavy flowers, like Queen Anne's lace, may be dried on a screen (the holes in the mesh have to be large enough to drop a stem though) so the stem can hang under the mesh. Petals or leaves can be laid out on a fine screen. It takes two to three weeks for most plants to dry.

Delicate flowers and leathery leaves may be dried in a desiccant. Choose from silicate gel, borax and white cornmeal, or borax and sand. If you choose silica gel, you will also need an airtight container. Sprinkle more over the flowers to cover them. Plants dried in a borax mixture need a wide, shallow box. Put a layer of desiccant in the bottom, then lay your flowers or leaves inside. Make sure they don't touch each other. It takes several days for most plants to dry in a desiccant.

How to Press Plants

Pressing works well for leaves and is the preferred method for herbs. Flat flowers such as pansies press well, too. Avoid fleshy stems or leaves, and flowers with bulky heads, as these rarely produce satisfactory results. Look at the three-dimensional plant and try to imagine how it will appear when pressed flat. Choose ones that suggest a pleasing pattern.

You can buy a commercial flower press with nifty clamp controls and special blotter paper. However, you can also dry plants by pressing them between sheets of paper and using some kind of weight. One effective method involves inserting leaves and flowers between the pages of old phone books. Stack the books several high for best results. Another method is to put the plants between layers of newspaper, then put a board on top, then a brick for weight. It takes three to four weeks for most plants to dry in a press.

Projects

Now that you know which plants to grow and how to prepare them, it's time to explore what you can do with them. Many crafts use dried flowers and herbs. These include three-dimensional displays, two-dimensional objects, and scented things.

Dried Bouquets

Everyone has seen dried bouquets. To make one, you need an opaque vase, a chunk of florists' foam, florists' wire, florists' tape, scissors, and an assortment of dried plant materials. Choose dried flowers for color and dried seedpods or grasses for texture. You may want harmonious colors, such as red blossoms with gold-painted pods; bold contrasts, such as purple statice and yellow strawflowers; or a monochromatic mix of bachelor's button, larkspur, and blue-dyed bunny tails.

Trim the florists' foam so that it fits snugly into the bottom of the vase. Arrange the flowers and seedpods into a balanced bouquet. Vary the heights of the heads by trimming the lower ends of the stems. Use florists' wire and tape, if needed, to adjust the shape of stems. Stick the stems firmly into the foam. The finished bouquet should have a domed or triangular profile, with good visual diversity.

Wreaths

Wreaths come in many styles. The core—usually made from grapevines, craft foam, raffia, or moss—provides support for the flowers and other decorations. Circular and heart-shaped wreaths are most popular, but others exist. Hang a wreath on your door or an inside wall. For this project you'll need to gather some materials.

Materials

> A wreath core
>
> Scissors
>
> Florists' wire
>
> Florists' tape
>
> Various dried plants (e.g., moss or baby's breath; strawflower for color; roses or gilded lotus pods)
>
> Hot glue gun

Trim all the stems to about 4 to 6 inches for bundling; or less than one inch if using a hot glue gun. Cut a short piece of wire to make a hook and attach it to the top of your wreath.

Start working on the right side of the wreath. Use florists' wire or tape to gather the plants into small bundles of filler with one or two bright flowers. Lay the first bundles on the right side of the wreath and wire them down.

If you're working with a glue gun, attach items in small areas similarly. Work counterclockwise so that new bundles cover the exposed stems of previous bundles.

When the wreath is full, look for the best places to put your special accents; the two o'clock and ten o'clock positions on a round wreath are good. You can also cradle a more complicated accent of several bunched flowers inside the bottom of the wreath.

Potpourri

Potpourri relies on scented herbs or essential oil for its fragrance, dried flowers for color, and dried seedpods for texture. Anise hyssop, lavender, marjoram, and rose all contribute their scents, and rosebuds look especially pretty in a blend. Consider pompon dahlia, globe, and button-shaped strawflowers, and yarrow for color. Poppy seedpods also look interesting, especially if they are dyed or painted.

For this project, you'll need some assorted herbs and flowers, a large bowl, orris powder or other fixative, and a small basket with a lid. Combine the plant materials in the bowl. Fluff them gently with your hands to mix everything together. Sprinkle orris powder into the mix to preserve the scent and fluff again. Scoop the potpourri into the basket, secure the lid, and place it where you want to enjoy the scent. It can be refreshed periodically with more herbs or essential oil.

Suncatchers

Pressed flowers may be arranged between a pane of glass and an opaque backing for a framed display, or between two panes of glass for a suncatcher. (Despite their name, it's best to display suncatchers in a north or interior window, because direct sun can fade dried flowers.) Blossoms like delicate Queen Anne's lace or bold-colored scarlet sage work best for these projects. Include some pretty foliage such as yarrow or bachelor's button.

Start with either a disassembled picture frame or two panes of glass and some copper edging film. Center the biggest, best flower on the glass. Arrange the other flowers and foliage in complementary positions. Then, press the backing, or the second pane, over the arrangement. Reassemble the picture frame, or put the edging film around the suncatcher, holding the arrangement firmly in place.

Bookmarks

A bookmark is a very simple project to make with pressed flowers. You can buy clear craft film made of archival materials that will last for many years, but you can also make a fine bookmark from clear packing tape. Cut one piece of film to the desired size. On that film, arrange two small flowers, or one flower and a sprig of foliage.

Cover with a matching piece of film, sticky sides together. Press to seal from the center outward, removing air bubbles as you go. Trim the edges. If you wish, punch a hole at the top and add a tassel.

Imagine the Future

Imagine a garden filled with colorful shapes and whimsical seedpods. When winter comes, the flowers will fade, the seeds will fall, and the garden will disappear under snow—except for the parts you have preserved. Indoors, pressed flowers will still bloom in suncatchers, and dried bouquets will beckon; potpourri will sweeten the air with memories of long summer days. In the end, time is the strangest magic of all, and with a little knowledge, you can make it do tricks for you.

Resources

Armitage, Allan M., and Judy M. Laushman. *Specialty Cut Flowers: The Production of Annuals, Perennials, Bulbs, and Woody Plants for Fresh and Dried Cut Flowers*. Portland, OR: Timber Press, 2003.

Becker, Jim and Dotti Becker. *An Everlasting Garden: A Guide to Growing, Harvesting, and Enjoying Everlastings*. Loveland, CO: Interweave Press, 1994.

Cunningham, Scott. *Cunningham's Encyclopedia of Magical Herbs*. St. Paul, MN: Llewellyn Publications, 1991.

DIY Network. "Pressed Flower Suncatcher," no author listed. Retrieved on July 30, 2008, at http://www.diynetwork.com.

Hillclimb Media. "Drying Flowers." Retrieved from http://www.gardenguides.com/how-to/tipstechniques/flowers/drying.asp.

Flowers, Diane. *Preserving Flowers: Dried & Pressed Floral Designs for Every Season*. New York: Sterling, 2008.

Hillier, Malcolm. *The Book of Dried Flowers: A Complete Guide to Growing, Drying, and Arranging*. New York: Simon and Schuster, 1987.

Jollands, Beverley. *Scented Potpourri and Floral Gifts*. Gifts from Nature Series. London: Southwater, 2004.

Nadeau, Alyce. *Making & Selling Herbal Crafts: Tips, Techniques, Projects*. New York: Lark Books, 1995.

Trinklein, David. "Drying Flowers and Foliage for Arrangements." University of Missouri, September, 2006. Retrieved from http://extension.missouri.edu/xplor/agguides/hort/g06540.htm.

"Learn to Make Potpourri," no author listed. Retrieved July 30, 2008 from http://www.ehow.com/how_325_create -dried-flower.html.

The World of Wildcrafting

⋙ by Susan Pesznecker ⋘

A woman strides along a path; she wears a broad straw hat and carries a deep basket. Every hundred feet or so, she stops and bends down to examine a plant. Occasionally, she takes a set of plant shears from her basket and snips off a few samples, which are delivered to the cool depths of her basket. Pulling a small notebook from the basket, she jots down notes, including the time, date, and a few details about the location. After a couple of hours, she heads home and spills her herbal treasures out onto her workspace, ready to add them to her apothecary. Welcome to the wildcrafter's world.

"Wildcrafting" means going out into nature to collect plants for magical, medicinal, or culinary use. It's one of the best ways to obtain fresh, potent, organic herbs, and it is an important practical skill for all budding herbalists. However, wildcrafters can't just head outside and start whacking away at the underbrush—they must master basic skills while also considering ethics and conservation in their wildcrafting practices.

Getting Started

All wildcrafting begins with a few basic materials:

Materials

Sturdy shoes

Sun hat

Lightweight long-sleeved shirt

Garden gloves

Sunscreen

Plant shears

A field guide for the plants in your area

Newspaper

Plastic bags, or other materials for temporary storage

Paper and pencil

A camera to take pictures of plants for identification at a later time

A basket to hold everything

Choosing a Location

When planning your outing, think about the wild areas around you. Do you have a local green space or wilderness park nearby? A Bureau of Land Management tract or a national forest? Maybe you own land yourself or have a friend with an expanse of natural space. Before venturing into a new space, always check to make sure you don't need special permissions or permits. Remember those ethics!

Do Your Research

Precede your trip with research. Find out what herbs grow nearby and identify local poisonous and endangered plants. Poisonous plants must be avoided, while rare plants must be protected and allowed to flourish.

Prepare Yourself

Speaking of flourishing, your emotional state affects your ability to find and identify plants, so wildcraft when you feel good and have a clear mind. Concerns, fatigue, and stress will cloud your awareness of the signs around you, leaving you likely to misstep or miss important signs. Many places of power are inaccessible without a proper emotional state. You must approach the Earth with openness and respect if you wish to learn from her.

Use Common Sense

Common sense is important, too. If you're heading out alone, be sure to file a "trip plan," letting someone else know where you'll be and when to expect you back. If you're alone, don't head too far off the beaten path. Keep in mind that something as simple as a turned ankle can strand a solo wildcrafter, and leave her unable to walk. If you get stuck and no one knows where you are, you've got a problem. Carry a cell phone, and if you're in a truly wild area, carry a small pack of survival gear that includes matches, fire starters, a flashlight, a first aid kit, food, water, a whistle, and a space blanket.

You may have a defined plan of action—perhaps heading to a spot where you know you'll find a specific stand of plants—or you may be exploring new territory. Go easy and observe as you walk. The biggest mistake beginning wildcrafters make is to get excited and start harvesting from the first patches they find. A better approach is to keep investigating, because a larger, healthier stand may be just around the next corner. And speaking of health: never harvest from within five hundred feet of a road or train track, as your herbs will be contaminated with toxins and even heavy metals. Also, ensure that your location hasn't been sprayed with herbicides.

Plan enough time for your wildcraft outing that you don't have to rush. Wildcrafting isn't just a matter of cutting plants. New experiences await you around every turn. Being in the outdoors puts you in touch with the natural world. Keep your eyes open wide so that you don't miss any of the lessons that Mother Earth has to offer.

Ethical Practices

The ethical wildcrafter wants to preserve the natural environment and ensure that a healthy supply of herbs continues to thrive in the wild. Herbs are part of our natural inheritance, and responsible wildcrafters follow a set of practices aimed at protecting wild stands and caring for the ecosystem as a whole. Always observe the "leave no trace" approach. Stay on trails. If you must venture off-trail, walk on bare areas or on large tracts of common undergrowth such as ferns, salal, and so forth. Avoid stepping on wildflowers or any plants known to be in short supply. Pack out all materials and garbage. Repair your harvesting sites, so no one will even suspect that you've been there.

Do your research. Avoid harvesting endangered plants, which are those species in danger of becoming extinct in the foreseeable future, or threatened plants that are likely to become endangered. Rare plants have small, localized populations. While they may not be listed as threatened or endangered because multiple populations are both stable and numerous, their spotty presence puts them at risk. Fragile plants are those that may suffer if their habitat is lost or altered. Plants that are endangered, threatened, rare, or fragile should not be wildcrafted. Check with your closest Department of Agriculture or Department of Fish and Wildlife for listings in your area.

Some locations may require you to obtain special permissions or a harvesting permit before your outing. Follow these guidelines carefully; they exist to protect wild plants.

The Harvest

Consider this Native American wisdom on gathering:

> *When gathering plants walk by the first seven.*
> *Leave the eighth for the animals.*
> *You may harvest the ninth.*

Here is a traditional gathering rhyme:

Pluck if you must one flower face
But leave ten others in its place.
Two feet square must hold this many;
Otherwise look, but don't pick any.

The message is clear: don't take too much! One of my mentors taught me an even tougher approach, telling me only to harvest one plant if there were two dozen in its place.

When gathering, consider these rules:

- Herbal properties are affected by the timing and method of their harvesting. Find out which parts of the plant to gather and what time of day is optimal for gathering.

- Don't gather during rainy weather, because damp weather leads to rot and mold.

- Harvest in a way that does as little harm as possible. Use shears or a blade to cut plants cleanly rather than rip them from the soil. Dig roots with a sharp trowel or spade.

- Harvest only what you can use. Many beginners tend to harvest by the armload, and their herbs end up in the compost pile.

- Harvest only as much as you can process. Working with herbs takes time. Some processes, like cleaning and slicing valerian root, can take hours of tedious work.

- Move around as you harvest. Harvesting from multiple parts of a stand will reduce your impact on the area.

- If the location is one you know, monitor the health of the stand over time. If the plant population drops, don't harvest for a period of time to allow it to recover.

Know the Growth Cycle of Plants before You Pick

Another important consideration in harvesting has to do with whether the plant is an annual, biennial, or perennial.

Annuals are plants that grow, produce seed, and die within a single growing season, and the plant's whole existence goes toward seed production. If you're harvesting the roots or leaves of annuals, gather them before the plant's flowering season. Gathering annual roots after the plants have flowered means that much of the plant's potency and resources have gone into the creation of flowers.

Biennial plants have a two-year life span. During the first year, the plant grows and develops a root system. During the second year, the plant develops flowers or fruits and then dies. Biennial roots should therefore be harvested during the first year of growth. If you wait until the plant's second year of life, most of its nutrient resources will have gone toward forming seeds. Biennial roots are usually gathered during autumn, winter, or early spring. If you collect roots during spring, gather them before the plant's energy begins to produce leaves and stems. Collect biennial leaves during the second growth year.

Perennial plants grow and produce seed for many years. Some live only for a few years, while others may live for decades. In general, the older plants have more potency in their roots for medicinal uses. Fall, winter, and early spring are good harvest times for perennial roots, as the plant goes dormant after the first frost, leaving much of the potency concentrated in the root system. Harvest perennial leaves before the plant flowers.

In general, gather whole herbs when the flower is forming but not yet opened; choose a dry morning. Gather the aerial parts: leaves, stems, and flowers. When gathering flowers for their essential oils alone, harvest just before the bud opens because younger flowers are usually more potent than mature flowers. Harvest mature leaves before the plant flowers. Always gather deciduous tree leaves before Summer Solstice, because after that they contain too much natural pesticide for human consumption.

Harvest fruits and berries when they are just barely ripe. If you wait until the fruit is robustly ripe, much of the nutrient value will be lost. Gather seed, seedpods, and fruit when they are mature, but before they drop from the plant.

To harvest bark, cut it from small branches or from the roots of a felled tree. Never remove the bark all around a tree (a practice known as "girdling"), because the tree will die.

Safe Gathering

Always ensure positive identification before taking any plant. The ideal situation is to work with a mentor who can teach you the plants and their languages. If working with a mentor isn't possible, invest in a good field guide for your local area. Books with actual photographs are better than those with sketches. Also, while it's fun to use common and folk names for plants, the serious wildcrafter knows the only way to positively identify each plant is by its Latin name.

Avoid potential toxic plants by doing careful research. Many dangerous plants resemble other safe ones, and if errors are made, the consequences can be serious. For instance, in northwestern Oregon, the death camas (*Zigadenus venenosus*) is almost identical to wild onion (*Allium*) species. Mistaking these two can be fatal! If you aren't sure of a plant, pass it by.

Processing the Herbs

After gathering, soak herbs and roots in a large bowl of water with a few teaspoons of vinegar or salt for 20 minutes—this removes insects and dirt. Rinse and drain well. Use food herbs immediately, or wrap them loosely in paper toweling and store in a tight plastic bag in the refrigerator. Use within a day for best flavor and nutrition.

To dry herbs for storage, allow them to air-dry on paper-lined trays in a warm room out of direct light. Don't dry medicinal or culinary herbs in the microwave, as this affects nutrients and essential oils. I don't put my herbs in a food dehydrator for the same reasons.

Store dried herbs in tightly closed glass jars out of direct light and in a cool place. Under these conditions, most herbs will remain potent for about a year. Some herbs, such as calendula blossoms and ginger rhizomes, may also be frozen whole.

Using the Herbs

Here are a few quick ideas for enjoying your spoils:

- Cook the leaves of spring violets as you would spinach, or use in salads.

- Use baby dandelion leaves in salads or steam them as a potherb.

- Add edible flowers such as forsythia blossoms, violets, Johnny-jump-ups, wisteria, and calendula to a salad.

- Pick red clover flowers and float them in soups, or add to salads.

- Prepare stovetop jam by gently boiling equal parts safe wild berries (e.g., Oregon grape, salmonberries) and sugar until the mixture gels, about 10 minutes.

- Steep 1 teaspoon fresh or dried herbs in 1 cup of freshly boiled water for 5 to 10 minutes. Sweeten your fresh tea with honey.

Congratulations on joining the world of wildcrafting. May your path be sure and your discoveries brilliant!

Rooted for Good Growth

☙ by JD Hortwort ☙

What a well-rounded education is for the Pagan gardener, a well-developed root system is for a plant. Just as in-depth study grounds the student, keeping him or her steady against the buffeting winds of life, so does the sturdy root system sustain a plant against whatever nature (or mankind) throws at it.

It's pretty obvious that roots anchor plants into the ground. Just try tugging a poke plant from the garden or a tuft of witch grass from the fencerow. But you've probably noticed that some plants seem to have hardly any root system. Periwinkle, also called sorcerer's violet, scampers across the ground, stopping every foot or so to

tickle the loose topsoil with a few creamy-white roots. Other plants, like the German bearded iris, have very curious root growth, at least in the south. The bearded iris tends to leave what look like thick fleshy roots right on top of the ground.

What Roots Do for Plants

While support is a main function of roots, another very important task of this plant part is to provide water and nutrients to the plant. So whether a plant has a long taproot (as is found on the poke plant) or a fibrous root system (like witch grass has), the root system provides the nutrients that sustain the plant through its life cycle.

Take a closer look at any plant root—get in really close and examine the root tip. What you should see coming off both the taproot and fibrous root system are little root hairs. The magic happens in the root hairs. Through a process of osmosis, plants absorb moisture from the surrounding soil. Hopefully, the nutrients that the plant needs to survive are suspended in that moisture.

Without getting too technical, osmosis occurs when moisture is absorbed or translocated through the root-hair cell walls. Then it moves up through the plant's vascular system to provide the essential nutrients the plant will use along with photosynthesis to create carbohydrates for growth. Most of the time, translocation works from the soil into the plant. However, when soil conditions are especially dry, the process can work in the other direction, stressing and even killing the plant.

A third function of roots is to provide a storage area for excess food. The stored food might sustain the plant in the next growing season or after it has been cut back by a grazing animal. Or it might be shuttled into the creation of an entirely new plant for the following season.

When is a Root not a Root?

This is where the study of plant roots gets a little tricky. When is a root not a root? When it is a specialized plant part. Remember those tap and fibrous roots mentioned earlier? They are the real thing, what biologists mean when they say "root." Roots can be the storage area for plants. But plants can have parts that seem to mimic roots. These parts are really specialized stems, usually intended for the storage of nutrients. These specialized stems include rhizomes, stolons, bulbs, tubers, and corms.

Rhizomes are specialized stems that run just below or right at the top of the soil surface. The German bearded iris mentioned earlier has a rhizome. The part of ginger that we use in herbal blends, or in teas, is a rhizome. The roots are the thinner parts that radiate off of the rhizome.

Stolons, on the other hand, are prostrate stems that run on top of the ground. Strawberries and white clover are good examples of this type of specialized system. This type of plant sends out a stolon that has a node on the end, and wherever the stem touches down, the node will root and a new plant is formed.

Bulbs, corms, and tubers are all specialized stems. If you have ever grown any of these in water, you've seen the roots that sprout from them that are meant to support the new plant. The swollen part is a storehouse of food for the next generation.

Regardless of the type of root system, they need room to grow. You may have seen plants that muscled their way up through hot concrete, or that cleaved to mountain boulders with only their roots. Plants are wonderfully persistent opportunists, which should be a comfort to the humans who can be so disrespectful of nonhuman life. But where roots can grow and where they should grow are two different things.

Wherever you live, make certain that the soil you plant in is loose and well drained. Some plants like a rich soil mixture; others prefer a leaner mix. Visit the library or the local cooperative extension office for information on growing specific plants. Local garden centers can also direct the gardener in the right way to work the soil to grow healthy root systems that will support healthy plants.

Hydrangeas: Timeless Beauties

❧ by Chandra Moira Beal ❧

Hydrangeas are familiar flowers; their large blooms bring flamboyant color to gardens around the world in late summer and autumn. They have a slightly old-fashioned feel (you might hear some people call them hortensia) and, indeed, the shrubs can live for many generations. Hydrangeas are true survivors and can often be seen flowering in overgrown or neglected gardens.

But hydrangeas are just as at home in the modern garden. They are ideal for framing a low window or decorating a plain wall. Use them in big, bold groups in a border, or even in large containers. They are easy to grow, dependable, will improve with age, and are suitable for all but the coldest climates. With their timeless appeal, hydrangeas can add grace and charm to cottage gardens and urban settings alike.

This genus of shrubs and climbers includes a wide variety of sizes, colors, shapes, and flower forms. Hydrangea flowers can look like delicate, lacy caps or robust mopheads. They can take the form of sturdy shrubs or evergreen climbers. A few are native to the Americas, but most come from East Asia. Some hydrangeas grow to just two feet, while others can reach towering heights of twenty feet or more. The foliage of some varieties produces autumn color, while others are variegated. A few cultivars will tolerate salt-laden winds in coastal areas.

The flower heads can be rounded, flat, or conical, and they come in all sizes. Most often you'll see two types of flowers: very small, fertile blossoms, or the sterile flowers known as ray florets, with three to five petals, usually about an inch across. The two main varieties we see today, mopheads and lacecaps, are part of the macrophylla species that is native to many parts of Asia. The mopheads have dome-shaped, rounded heads of large flowers that mainly consist of ray florets. The lacecap variety has a flat flower head with a large number of fertile flowers surrounded by sterile ray florets, giving it a delicate, lacy look.

If the blooms on your hydrangeas are pink, purple, or blue, it is likely you have a mophead or lacecap. In general, mophead and lacecap leaves are relatively thick and crisp, somewhat shiny and oval and have a rough-toothed edge. Stems often have tiny black or red streaks or speckles. If the blooms on a plant are white, it could be any type hydrangea and will grow in the same conditions.

Planting and Care Tips

When planning where to plant your hydrangeas, choose a location that is about four by four feet so the plants can reach full size without being pruned. Use the pots they came in as a guide for how to deep to plant them. All hydrangeas will bloom and grow well in morning sun and afternoon shade, but the farther north you live, the more sunlight hydrangeas need. No hydrangea will do well in heavy, constant shade, such as under a tree. Too much shade will cause the blooms to be sparse and not fully developed.

Mopheads and lacecaps prefer dappled shade against a north- or west-facing wall. If it is too bright, however, they are likely to scorch. Plants also need to be sheltered from cold winds, which can damage new foliage during the spring.

Hydrangeas need well-drained soil, and plenty of moisture during the summer. But never over water them, especially in clay soil, as this can lead to root rot. Apply mulch to drier soils to lock in moisture and promote decent-size flowers.

Plant hydrangeas in the early summer or late fall, well clear of any danger of frost. If you are going to transplant a hydrangea, wait until it has become dormant and lost all of its leaves (late fall or winter).

Hydrangeas respond well to fertilization once or twice in the summer. This can be as simple as adding something organic, such as manure or compost, to the soil. Stop fertilizing after August, and let your hydrangeas begin preparing for dormancy. Fertilizing at this time may stimulate new growth that will be too tender to survive the winter.

The acidity of the soil determines the color of the flowers. Intense blue flowers are grown in acidic soil and pink blossoms result from neutral or alkaline soil. It is possible to change the flower color from pink to blue, although the results won't compare with plants growing naturally in acid soil. It is much easier to change a hydrangea from pink to blue, which entails adding aluminum to the soil, than it is from blue to pink, where you have to take aluminum out of the soil or out of reach of the hydrangea.

Some varieties do well in containers, and it is easier to control and alter the pH of the soil in a container. Fill with lime-free compost and use a supplemental liquid food that contains a bluing compound. The liquid food is usually available at garden centers.

Hydrangeas may even change color on their own after they are planted or transplanted and have adjusted to the new environment. It is not unusual to see several different colors on one shrub the year following planting.

Pruning hydrangeas is not essential, but it does help to control their shape and can encourage a profusion of big, showy flowers each year. Without pruning, hydrangeas will continue to bloom, but the overcrowded stems will reduce the size of the flower heads.

At the end of summer or autumn, it is best to leave the faded flower heads on the shrub as protection against frost until the following spring. (And the brown papery domes look beautiful when covered with frost.) When spring returns, cut back the weak-looking, old, or diseased shoots down to the lowest bud. Shorten the remaining healthy stems to a strong bud.

Hydrangeas can live for many years. When they are at least five years old and well established, about a third of the older living stems can be pruned down to the ground each summer. Remove the older, less productive stems and cut back old flowering stems to a strong pair of buds. This will revitalize the plant and you should get a nice display of new flowers.

If your species is the type that flowers on the new season's wood, you can encourage more flowers by pruning the previous season's growth in late winter or early spring to two or three pairs of buds. If you want to produce larger shrubs with smaller flowers, cut back the previous year's flowering shoots by half to two-thirds in late winter or early spring. Prune climbing species only to keep them close to the wall.

Start Your Own Hydrangeas

Hydrangeas are fairly easy to root. In late summer, take a semi-ripe cutting from a branch of the shrub about five to six inches long. Most experts say the cutting will work best if taken from a branch that did not flower the same year. Remove the lower leaves and cut the largest leaves down to about half their size. Insert the cutting into damp vermiculite, coarse sand, or another sterile medium. Water the pot well and allow it to drain. Make sure the soil is moist but not soggy. Some people have had luck with simply rooting the branch in a glass or vase of water. Place cuttings in bright light, but never in direct sunlight. Cuttings should begin to form roots in two to three weeks, depending on temperature and humidity. If the cutting resists a tug with fingers, it is rooting.

If you take cuttings to overwinter and grow out the next spring, start them early in the summer to give them the best chance for surviving the winter. While some people manage to grow cuttings indoors through the winter, hydrangeas generally do best if grown outdoors. To protect them from the cold, sink the potted cuttings into the ground and cover them well with lightweight mulch, or put smaller pots of cuttings next to a foundation and cover them with large clay pots for the winter.

Control Those Garden Pests

Hydrangeas tend be relatively pest-free, but they can be visited by red spider mites, capsid bugs, aphids, and vine weevils. Hydrangea scale may also be an occasional problem. Very alkaline soil causes chlorisis. These conditions can typically be treated organically and won't harm the shrub in the long term.

Enjoy Blossoms Year Around

Dried hydrangea blossoms can lend a rustic, elegant look to a room. While it is tempting to cut the hydrangea blossoms for drying at the height of their color, the fresh, recently opened blooms rarely dry well in the open air. Hydrangeas preserve best when they are allowed to dry on the plant to a papery texture before picking. Leave blooms on the shrub until late summer, when the petals will begin to age and take on a vintage look. If left on the shrub a while longer, many blooms will pick up interesting shades of burgundy and pink, especially in warmer climates. In the cooler climates, they may age to shades of blue and purple. Experiment with harvesting from August through October.

You can simply cut the blooms, strip off the leaves, arrange them in a vase (with or without water) and leave them to dry. It is not necessary to hang hydrangeas upside down to dry unless the stems are very thin and weak.

Hydrangeas are low maintenance friends in the garden that provide a bounty of beauty. Enjoy your hydrangeas year-round and for many generations to come.

Save Your Seeds: It's Easy and Fun

❧ by JD Hortwort ❧

You have planned and maybe even started your garden, and you have anticipated the herbal teas, potpourris, and medicines you'll soon be harvesting. But have you considered that your spring garden could be the source of another sort of gift? Almost every plant makes collectible seeds. Collecting them ensures future harvests for you; it can also mean perfect presents for your gardening friends and neighbors.

Seeds are created at the base of most flowers. Those seeds can be as fine as dust or as large as a coconut! Basically, they are all little envelopes of life complete with a genetic plan for growth, a few carbohydrates to kick start the process, and a coating to ensure everything stays safe until conditions are right for growth. Your job as a seed gatherer is to pick this little package at the right time and then protect it once you gather it.

First, whether you are collecting food seeds or ornamentals, harvest seeds from only the healthiest plants. Another good tip is to collect seeds from a variety of plants, not just one. This practice is a good protection in case one plant has produced inferior seeds.

Also, bear in mind that the latest flower or vegetable from the store may be a hybrid. Hybrids result from mechanical, or human-assisted, pollination. Plants produced from seeds gathered from a hybrid variety will not be like the parent plant. It will revert to characteristics of one or the other of the grandparents. Check with the garden center assistant if you're not sure or do some research with your local Cooperative Extension office to find out if the plant you are purchasing is a hybrid.

If you are harvesting seeds from annuals, biennials, and perennials, harvest them after the flower has faded. Obviously, this isn't true in the case of many garden vegetables. For example, if you pick a squash after the flower has faded, you'll get a tasty side dish but no seeds mature enough to save. So, we'll come back to garden seeds in just a moment.

In the case of flowers, though, seeds are ready when the petals fall or the tops have taken on that puffy look. Think about the way a brown-eyed Susan (*Rudbeckia*) looks when the yellow petals are gone. You have a stiff brown globe, but where are the seeds? Or consider basil. The flower may be gone, but the seeds aren't obvious.

When you want to harvest seeds that you can't see, or small seeds, paper bags come in handy. Collect the dried flower stalk and put it head down into the bag. Set it in a warm, dry place and check it in a day or two. If you shake the bag vigorously, you'll find the seeds drop readily from their hiding place.

Seed aren't always hidden. Sunflower seeds, for example, are large and obvious in the center of the blossom. All you have to do is let the flower head dry and shuck out the seeds. If the weather isn't cooperating, collect the flower and hang it upside down in a warm dry spot until it completes the drying process. This works well for any flowering plant.

Now, for those garden vegetables. Selecting beans, peas, okra, and corn seeds that are ready to save is pretty easy. Once the pod of beans, peas, and okra has turned tan or brown, the seed is ready. In the case of corn, the seeds are ready to harvest when the husks are dry and brown.

Collecting seeds from leaf crops (greens and lettuce, etc.) or from root crops (beets, carrots, and radishes, etc.) is easy, too. All of these plants produce flowers at the end of their life cycle. Once the flower has faded, the seedpod is left. Wait for that to dry and—voilà!—you have seeds.

But what about melons, squash, or gourds seeds that can't be seen? Melon seeds are ready when the fruit is ready. Gather the seeds, wash them off in a 10 percent bleach solution (1 ounce bleach to 10 ounces water) and then spread them on newspaper or a plate until they are dry.

With cucumbers or squash, you have to be patient. Let the cucumber get as big as it will and then turn yellow. With squash, leave it on the plant until the outer skin gets hard. Then, whether you are collecting cukes or squash, treat them like you would the melon seeds.

Tomatoes are a bit trickier. You'll need to scoop out the seeds and let the whole mess ferment in a covered container for two to three days. Then dump it all in a jar of water, shake it up and let it all settle out. The good seeds will sink to the bottom of the jar. Pour off the top gunk. Rinse the seeds with cool water and then spread them out on newspaper or wax paper to dry.

Regardless of which type of seeds you are saving, they must be kept dry until planting time. The time-honored way to save seeds is in paper envelopes. Sealable glass jars work well, but plastic bags are not a good idea, because plastic tends to trap moisture. However, there's nothing wrong with putting your seeds in envelopes and *then* putting the envelopes in a plastic container to keep everything dry.

The last big question is whether to refrigerate or not refrigerate. Refrigeration isn't absolutely necessary for storing seeds. All you need is a cool dark place. Of course, you can store the seeds in a sealed container in the back of the refrigerator. Some studies indicate that for every 10 degrees Fahrenheit decrease in storage temperature, up to but not actually crossing into freezing, you can double the storage life of your seeds.

Make Decorations and Gifts

Now that you have your treasures, gift some seeds to friends, and include a photo if you have access to a digital camera and a printer.

Seeds can become Yule or Winter Solstice decorations, too. Purchase inexpensive, hollow tree ornaments and some beeswax. Portion your seeds into the ornaments. Add a little paper tag with the name of the seed and the date it was collected. Soften the wax and make little plugs for the opening. Insert the ornament hook immediately and let the wax set up. Then, hang the ornament on your tree, or let your guests pick one to take home.

Whether you are using them as gifts or saving them yourself, preserving your own seeds is a rewarding and satisfying way to expand your love of gardening.

Variety is the Herb, or Spice, of Life

by Carole Schwalm

When it comes to land-scaping, herbs are every bit as versatile as any flower, shrub, or grass. Don't tell anyone, but mix them in with the regular spring nursery infusion of "normal" plants, without identifying tags, you can't tell the difference.

Herbs come with large leaves, fine and feathered leaves, delicate blooms and in various colors. They offer both annual and perennial choices. There are shade lovers and sun lovers. You can opt for short, medium, and tall herbs, or all of the above. Herbs are super hardy and almost pest free. There's something for every space and garden. You don't even need a design. Just strew the seeds to recreate their natural state.

Fill in bare spots on your lawn with herbs like thyme, or mint that grows like kudzu (a coarse, twisting plant). Take a walk on the wild side, a step beyond the ordinary, and plant chives or garlic with roses, rosemary with daisies, or dill with iris. The show goes on even after the flowers finish blooming.

Do you buy geraniums or petunias for the planters on each side of your front door? Add some sweet basil, a dark opal-colored plant with lovely pink flowers that grows to 18 inches tall. Plant the sweet basil in the middle of the container and add a couple of thyme plants near the edge. In time, the thyme cascades down the side, while the basil reaches skyward. Alter your mindset, expand your imagination and, presto, you magically have both a flowering plant and ingredients for pesto.

Sweet basil and cilantro in a flue tile make a beautiful and prolific couple. Fit them snugly in a bare corner somewhere. It is perfectly legal, although it flies in the face of tradition, to have herbs peeking through mulch. Enhance your flower garden, flowerpots, and window boxes with chives, green onions, or feathery dill. Strew the seeds and recreate their natural state.

A long, long time ago, herbs grew wild. The artists of the Lascaux cave paintings of herbal plants (carbon dated 13,000 to 25,000 BCE) walked through fields, intrigued by the aroma of the plant's volatile oils. Nature's gifts of anise, cardamom, coriander, cumin, dill, saffron, sesame, and poppy inspired people not only to use them, but to record them in ancient cuneiform. Native Americans used the anise, lavender, parsley, sorrel, watercress, and wild leeks that once flourished in natural abundance.

But time marched beyond this lovely existence. The fields of flowers, and the beautiful shades of green and other colors, shrank. Herbs became spoils of war and objects of trade. Between 660 and

1200 BCE, herbs were only available to the wealthy. Peppercorns were used as currency during a coin shortage. Emperors, even the church, controlled herbal farming in Europe. They were literally the color of money.

Kitchen gardens existed until herb and spice jars became business and appeared on grocer's shelves. Those aromatic, beautiful, delicious, hardy plants have been tamed.

It is time now to take a deep breath and alter your mindset; go back to the future and add the word "herbscaping" to your personal dictionary.

Herbs are lovely, hardy, multipurpose plants. In addition to turning food flavors up a notch, they have colorful flowers and leaves. And, lucky you, if you've walked outside early in the morning and experienced the perfume of morning dew or afternoon sun on rosemary, or you've stepped lightly and discovered the scent from the thyme meandering its way along your flagstone walk, you already know about some herbal virtues.

Herbs are Mother Nature's natural air freshener. Basil, rosemary, and wormwood are Mother Natures' natural pest control, repelling ants and flies. Accentuate your garden spaces by selecting short, medium, and tall herbs from the list below to plant. Use the short or medium as companions to leggy plants with sparse leaves, and use the spreading tall varieties to make lovely backdrops for any area.

Short Herbs
Portulaca

Portulaca, or moss rose, is an annual that withstands drought and heat. The plant has fleshy, reddish-colored stems and bright-colored flowers. It makes a nice border plant, and is lovely in a rock garden.

Thyme

Thyme is the shortest of the short herbs. It has tight little leaves and even smaller flowers, and the more you prune and use thyme, the more it produces. This is actually the case when it comes to any of the herb (or spice) plants.

Woodruff

Woodruff is low and fast-spreading, which makes an excellent ground cover. The tiny white flowers smell like new-mown hay when you walk on them.

Medium Herbs

Medium-size means that the plant grows to around 12 inches tall. They make good fillers for the center of a garden bed, or they can be placed toward the back in a narrow garden.

Anise

Anise has fine, serrated leaves and small, whitish flowers that contain the seeds. The umbels are 3 inches in diameter. Anise does well in dry climates. If you want double the pleasure and double the herbs, plant anise and coriander together.

Chives

Chives are grasslike, have pretty purple flowers, and are veritable stars when it comes to filling in blanks in window boxes. This hardy perennial makes a nice border plant; it likes rock gardens, too.

Green Spearmint

Green spearmint spreads rapidly and can be invasive, but it smells wonderful. Use it to add nice texture to the garden.

Lavender

Lavender plants have gray-green leaves and lovely flowers. The plants make a stunning backdrop, and act like a wonderful natural air freshener when planted outside an open window.

Marjoram

Marjoram grows to at least 18 inches. This perennial is one to keep in mind if you envision a beautiful cascading plant or a spreading border.

Parsley

Parsley is not just a restaurant garnish, but we all know that! Basil, marjoram, and parsley together form a trio of prolific companion plants.

Purslane

Purslane is a fast-growing succulent that falls into the category of edible landscaping. It literally "grows like a weed."

Summer Savory

Summer savory has abundant, but delicate, bronze leaves, and it produces either white or lavender flowers.

Tall Herbs

Tall herbs reach from 2 feet up to 6 feet tall. When placed in a narrow bed, tall herbs can look awkward unless they are accompanied by a pole, or something that will help them look more like a structural element in the garden.

Borage

Borage has pink, star-shaped flowers, and it is so prolific once started that it sows itself. The flowers are edible and are often used as a garnish. Bees love borage.

Caraway

Caraway has feathery leaves that resemble carrot-tops and cream-white clusters of flowers. The caraway clan doesn't like the dill clan, so don't plant them too close together.

Cardamom

Cardamom (a spice) grows 8 to 10 feet tall. The leaves are wide and shiny green, and the flowers lie on or close to the ground.

Catnip

Catnip has grayish leaves and purple, pink, or white flowers. Needless to say, cats love it.

Chervil

Chervil has lacy, sea-green leaves and white flowers. Chervil and radishes are prolific companion plants, and the former beautifies a sometimes-straggly latter.

Chicory

Chicory can grow quite tall. The perennial plant has blue flowers. It is also drought resistant.

Coriander

Coriander, edible from the root to the flower, still grows wild in Europe. The flowers are either white or purple. This plant does not like humidity.

Dill

Dill has feathery leaves and yellowish blooms that are the source of dill seeds. Dill and onion are prolific companion plants. Bees love dill just as much as people and pickles do.

Fennel

Fennel has light, feathery, green leaves. It grows quite tall and is drought hardy. Basil and dill are friendly companion plants to fennel, and butterflies love it.

Garlic and Onions, the "Holy Duo"

If Creole chefs call the onions, celery, and a bell pepper mire-poix the "holy trinity," garlic and onions are the "holy duo." Virgil and Homer wrote glowingly of garlic's virtues.

A member of the allium family, garlic gets along well with other flowers and vegetables. Garlic rewards you with "flowers," which are actually miniature cloves of the plant. Not everyone likes garlic, though. Horace considered it vile, vulgar, and "more poisonous than hemlock." If you are like Horace, think of your flowers. Roses especially benefit, and garlic is a natural aphid deterrent.

Onions, a grasslike fill-in, add green color and interesting height to flower beds or containers. The leaves turn brown in time, which simply means that your crop is ripe for harvest. It takes 100 days to grow onions from onion sets, compared to 120 days to grow them from seed. They like at least ten hours of sunlight.

Ginger

Ginger grows tall and has spiky leaves, causing it to resemble a cornstalk. It grows slow and often doesn't flower during the first two years. This plant loves humidity!

Hyssop

Hyssop forms spikes of either purple or white flowers. The plants make beautiful borders or edgings; it likes warm weather, and dry soil conditions. Bees and butterflies like it.

Oregano

Oregano is an attractive little shrub that still grows wild on hillsides in Europe. It even grows in poor soil. It rewards you with either pink or white flowers.

Peppermint

Peppermint has reddish stems with pink or purple flowers. This one is easy to grow. It thrives anywhere, with little care. It is also drought resistant. There are three thousand five hundred varieties from which to choose.

Paprika

Paprika is shrublike and produces pods. Paprika is worthy of getting to know more about. Yes, it really does have a flavor.

Rosemary

Rosemary is shrublike and fills a container nicely. It vines down over the sides or can be staked to stand tall. Rosemary does flower. You can also try your hand at topiary.

Sage

Sage grows quickly. Its gray-green leaves and bluish flowers look awesome behind a grouping of marigolds.

Sesame

Sesame has whitish leaves and pink flowers. Sesame does not branch and can be planted close together.

Tarragon

Tarragon has delicate leaves and is excellent for background fill-in. Some gardeners think it isn't beautiful, but that's all in the eye of the beholder, isn't it? Tarragon and vegetables are prolific companion plants that make each other look good.

Valerian

Valerian, or heliotrope, blossoms are small and can be crimson, pink, or white. Valerian blooms occur June through September and have a scent that is similar to the aroma of cherry pie, although some say the leaves smell like a smelly sock. Cats adore it, just as they do catnip, often ending up with the essence of both on their fur.

Herbal Economics 101

Now, let's move to the economics. In general, most seed packets cost under $2. Do the math: A 100-foot row of sweet Spanish onion seeds yields 55 pounds of onions for consumption, storage, and/or herbscaping. At the same per seed packet cost, thyme seeds (with each seed producing a plant) will edge your sidewalk at a minimal cost compared to the $2, or more, per plant that you will pay at the nursery.

Save on Dried Herbs

Depending on the product you buy, you can pay from $0.99 to $3.99 for a 2-ounce container of herbs. If you grow, dry, and store your personal stash, you can save money. The *pièce de résistance* is that they continue to beautify your yard and flower containers. Some herbs freeze well and still retain flavor. You can make pesto, gourmet oils, and vinegars for your personal use or to give as gifts.

Hopefully, you have arrived at the end of this article with a new mindset. Herbs are multipurpose, not just designed to flavor your cooking pot. They are as worthy of garden space as flowers and shrubs. Some are flowers and shrubs in their own right, and the more you snip through the season, the more these plants grow.

Tips on Starting Your Seedlings

Use good soil with drainage. You can mix with sand to start. Many are small seeds and should be planted shallow. Mist with water to start with, or they will wash away. You can start them in the house at the south or west window, or use grow lamps.

Resources

There are more than forty million search results for herbs on the Internet, and here are some of my favorites.

www.backyardgardener.com

www.BellaOnline.com

www.ehow.com

www.garlic-central.com

www.mccormicscienceinstitute.com

www.wvu.edu

Herbs in Winter

❧ by Suzanne Ress ❧

If you've taken the time to plant a herb garden in the spring, you've surely been rewarded with fresh herbs to pick all summer and into early fall. What could be more delicious than freshly plucked basil and marjoram sprinkled liberally over vine-ripened tomatoes? Or a very special salad made of nasturtium leaves and flowers, lovage, burnett, borage, and parsley? Or roasted chicken and potatoes with fresh rosemary and thyme? Or a sprig of fresh mint in a glass of iced tea? Or fresh chopped tarragon and chives on scrambled eggs? Or a gloriously colorful bouquet made up of shiso leaves, sage leaves and flowers, fennel flowers, rue leaves, garlic

chive flowers, and bee balm flowers given as an aromatic gift to a lucky friend?

Once the Autumn Equinox has passed and nighttime temperatures sink, the herbs in your garden will greatly slow down or stop growing. The annuals will lose their foliage and die, and many of the perennials will also lose their foliage and appear to die. Do not lose heart! With careful planting and planning, you can continue to enjoy your herbs and appreciate the special beauty of a sleeping herb garden all through the winter months.

During the growing season, roughly from May through September, you can collect herbs to preserve for use in winter.

Picking and Preserving Herbs

Herbs are at their peak "balsamic time," or aromatic potency, just before flowering, so watch them daily. The best time to cut or pick herbal foliage is in the morning of a dry day, after the dew has evaporated, but before the sun is high and hot. Picking herbal foliage during its growing season will actually make your plants grow thicker and more luxurious, so always pick more than you need for immediate use, and preserve the extra for winter.

If you grow fennel, once the yellow umbels begin to bloom, cut some of them off and dry them. You can use a small amount of dried fennel pollen to give a delicate licorice flavor to fish dishes, salads, and vegetables all year long.

Freezing

Other edible herbal flowers, such as borage, rose petals, nasturtium, and elderberry, can be frozen whole into ice cubes for a little touch of springtime right around the Winter Solstice.

Many, but not all, herbs freeze well. You can prepare cleaned, air dried, mini portions of fresh basil, chives, dill, fennel, lovage, parsley, mint, tarragon, oregano, and thyme for winter enjoyment, too. Seal the herbs in small, clearly labeled plastic freezer bags or containers and freeze. Don't try freezing woolly-leaved herbs like sage, lambs' ears or borage.

Add to Oil

Tender-leaved herbs, such as parsley, basil, pineapple sage, shiso, rue, and chives are preserved best when placed in olive (or other) oil. Chop the leaves or keep them whole, and store them completely covered by oil in closed glass jars at room temperature. Herbs preserved this way maintain their fresh flavor for months.

Drying

Drying herbs is time consuming, and the process can take up a lot of space, but to have dried herbs always at hand in the kitchen is worth it.

You can dry herbs the old-fashioned way by spreading them out on paper towels or cotton dish towels in a light, well ventilated place out of direct sunlight for two weeks, or until the leaves can be easily crumbled between two fingers. Do not leave them drying too long or they will draw dust. Alternatively, small bunches of herbs can be tied together with string and hung upside down from the rafters of a well-ventilated room. This looks very charming, though, and you might be tempted not to take them down even well after they've dried.

Tarragon, sage, dill, marjoram, rosemary, mint, thyme, shiso (beefsteak plant), and costmary all dry well. But don't bother with chives, cilantro, or parsley, because they fade to tan or yellow and lose their flavor and scent.

Herbs can also be dried on a paper-lined tray in a warm (200°F.) oven with the door left open a crack. They must be checked and turned often. Most will dry in twenty to thirty minutes, or less.

Once your herbs are dry, remove and discard the stems or stalks. Place the leaves, either whole or crumbled, in clean glass jars with tight-fitting lids. Store your herbs in a cool, dry place out of direct sunlight. They will maintain their aromas and flavors for up to a year, although herbs are at their best if used within six months.

Everyday Practical Ways to Store Herbs

Crumbled, dried herbs and extra seeds can also be stuffed into very small pillows made of muslin or pretty cotton calico, to put into drawers or closets as sachets. Dried lavender and southernwood sachets will keep moths at bay. Dried hops and chamomile flower sachets can be kept on a bedside table as a gentle sleep aid.

You can string a tiny, dried herb-stuffed bag on a fine silk or leather cord for use as a special necklace. These are especially nice to wear in winter when fingering the little bag around your neck releases a wonderful aromatic herb scent. Fennel seed, dried mint leaves, and thyme are good choices for these.

Whole (not crumbled) dried herbs on stems and stalks can be combined with small branches of evergreen (holly, pine, or fir) and perhaps a single silk rose in winter holiday floral arrangements. For a very festive look, you can use silver, gold, or opalescent white spray paint on dried herbs, seed heads, and pine cones to give them a more decorative look. Adding glitter is easy, too. Apply a thin coat of glue that will dry transparent to the dried items and then sprinkle with glitter to make your own holiday arrangements.

Bring Herbs in the House

More than a few herbs can be brought into the house for winter. Once they have finished blooming, carefully dig up the plant, being careful to keep roots intact. Place the plant in a pot or vase and cover the roots with the appropriate kind of soil.

Some herbs, such as chives and lemon grass, can be divided into smaller plants. You will need to dig up and untangle a portion of roots from the whole mass of roots. Then, transplant that section and you will have a whole new plant.

With other herbs, such as savory and hyssop, you can snip off several stalks close to the ground and bury the cut ends in potting soil, where, if kept moist, they will develop their own roots and make new plants.

Before doing any of this, though, make sure that your plants will not bring aphids into your house with them. To avoid this problem, spray the foliage for two or three days beforehand with a mild solution of dishwashing liquid and water. Do the transplanting in the morning on a sunny, dry day. Make sure that the plant's roots are well watered, and the transplant soil, as well as the potting soil, is moist and nutrient rich.

Herbs that usually don't mind being brought indoors for the winter are basil, oregano, mint, cilantro, thyme, rosemary, incense (*Plectranthus forsteri*), horehound, shiso, cardamom, ginger, and lemon grass. Feel free to experiment with other herbs as well.

Once brought inside, keep your potted herb plants in a cool place that is free of drafts, preferably next to, but not touching, a large south-facing window. Indoor plants need at least five hours of light a day to survive, so if you cannot provide them with natural light, use florescent tube lighting or a grow light. Keep your potted herbs in shallow trays (the kind you can get at the garden center). Water the trays, not the plants, daily, to keep the roots moist and help prevent the growth of fungi. Every now and then, use a very fine-nozzled spray bottle to mist the plants' leaves. Use your fresh indoor herbs all winter in food preparation! Regular snipping will encourage new growth.

Protect Perennial Herbs

For perennial herbs that will remain outdoors during the cold season, there are various things you can do to ensure their survival to the next spring. Trim away any dead, brown foliage from soft-stemmed plants. Prune off stray or dead stalks from woody-stemmed herbs like rosemary, wormwood, lavender, and sage. Do not go overboard with your pruning, though. Only take off what is necessary, or you might end up killing the plant! Certain woody-stemmed plants, such as lemon verbena and southernwood, are very sensitive to fall pruning and seem to do better if left shaggy all winter and then cut back in the early spring.

Mediterranean herbs, like rosemary, sage, lavender, and thyme, all benefit from having several large rocks placed behind and around them on the ground. Ideally, the rocks should be put down in midsummer and be south-facing to receive maximum hours of direct sunlight. The rocks will absorb and hold the sun's heat, keeping the air and ground temperature around the plant warm enough to survive even quite cold winter temperatures. This is an ancient method used in viticulture in lower alpine regions.

Mulch can be applied to herb gardens just before the ground freezes or immediately following the first freeze. Spreading several layers of newspaper over the ground and right up close to the base of each plant is a simple and effective mulch that will keep your herbal beds warm through winter. Place rocks at key points to prevent the wind from carrying away the newspapers, and then spread about a 2-inch layer of dried, fallen leaves over all. Fast-decomposing leaves, such as birch, are best, but whatever you rake up from your yard or the woods will do. With rain, snow, and temperature changes, this mulch should be about 75 percent decomposed by the following spring, at which time you can turn the rest, mixing it into the soil for a great nutrient and earthworm boost.

Some herbs cannot stand cold temperatures, but they are also difficult to transplant. I have managed to keep three large healthy stevia plants alive outdoors through two hard winters by covering them, shortly before the first frost, with heavy sheets of clear plastic. Wrap the plastic around the plant or plants, tape it closed with duct tape, and weigh down the bottom edge with rocks. Leave an opening along one side for air circulation. Heavy snows may cause the plants to fall down onto their sides. If that happens, brush the snow off the plastic and prop the plants back up. In the early spring, when you take off the plastic, the plants will look dead. Cut off all the brown parts and soon enough new green growth will appear.

Another possible solution for delicate herbal plants that don't like to be moved is a glass or Plexiglas cold frame, something like a mini greenhouse. You can buy a simple kit at a garden center or make your own.

Depending upon your USDA hardiness zone, you may find that there are a number of herbs that don't go completely into dormancy and will continue to be usable all winter. You can continue to pick and use the leaves of all kinds of sage, with the exception of pineapple sage, throughout the cold months, in temperature zones as low as 5 or 6, if you use reflective solar heat from rocks and mulching. Rosemary, thyme, oregano, santolina, and bay will all continue to provide you with aromatic flavors through the winter if they are treated well. Even parsley, which actually prefers cooler temperatures, will stay green and growing right up until the first frost, and sometimes beyond.

There are some herbs that bloom between the Winter Solstice and Spring Equinox, and these can really help cheer up your garden. Hellebore, also called Christmas rose, doesn't usually flower as early as Christmas, but rather in late January and even through heavy snow! These poisonous evergreen herbal plants produce lovely scentless blossoms in colors ranging from dark red, to pink and white, and pale green.

Comfrey flowers in early February, as does the wonderfully fragrant witch hazel tree. Wild violet and primrose are two more cheery little herbal plants that usually bloom as soon as the snow melts.

Aside from its continued usefulness throughout winter, your herb garden can also offer a unique and austere kind of beauty. It reminds us of the continuous life cycle, not only of herbs, but of other plants, animals, and human beings, as well. Winter gardens can look magical, especially early in the morning with a sparkling of frost over all.

You may choose not to be too thorough in your autumn trimming and pruning, and leave on some, or even most, of the dried, brown seed heads. Purple coneflower seed heads look like tiny hedgehogs on stalks. Fat tan or black poppy seed heads, the light brown spires of hyssop seed heads, and the medium-brown, cloud-shaped seed heads of yarrow, all add a fascinating sense of beautiful decrepitude to the winter herb garden. Umbel-shaped seed clusters like fennel, dill, wild carrot, coriander, and caraway look stark and witchy in their winter clothes. Globe-shaped angelica, papery balls of chive, garlic chive seed heads, and the dried, beige, fragrant blossoms of hops seem like ghostly reminders of their summertime selves. Amaranth flowers, when spent and brown, put one in mind of thick cobwebs. Tarragon, feverfew, horehound, and bee balm (bergamot) each take on a look of spindly nakedness that would seem to epitomize the word death, but all have their own peculiar beauty.

There are a few herb plants that remain evergreen, or silvery-green, throughout the winter. Sage, if your temperature zone permits it, maintains its downy, silver-gray foliage all year long. So does evergreen rosemary, with its fresh, piney fragrance, santolina (lavender cotton), the camphor-scented southernwood, and the soothing evergreen bay tree.

Your untrimmed herb garden may look very brown, with touches of silvery gray and greenish-silver and somber green in winter. But in its diminished glory, and with its wealth of seeds, tangled vines and stalks, fallen leaves, and warm dry ground cover, your winter garden will make a wonderfully rich feeding place and shelter for birds, small mammals, and reptiles. To everything there is a season, but in its down time you can still reap the benefits of your herb garden.

Culinary
Herbs

Le Fee Verte: Dancing with the Green Fairy

∼ by Laurel Reufner ∼

S hall we flirt with the Green Fairy for a while? There are rumors that she promises many gifts—clearness of thinking, enhanced creativity, and the gift of flowing poetry—if you'll only embrace her. She'll be your lover and your muse. Just ask the Bohemian artistes who populated Paris in the nineteenth century, many of whom died destitute from alcoholism and mental illness. Their Green Goddess exacted a powerful toll for her visions.

Absinthe was even more popular by the turn of the twentieth century. Oscar Wilde, Charles Baudelaire, Paul Verlaine, Henri de Toulouse-Lautrec, Vincent van Gogh, Henri

Matisse, and Édouard Manet all called absinthe their muse at some point. Even Ernest Hemingway worshipped the Green Goddess, buying his absinthe in Spain after it was banned in the United States.

Mr. Wilde described the effects of absinthe as such:

After the first glass, you see things as you wish they were. After the second, you see things as they are not. Finally, you see things as they really are, and that is the most horrible thing in the world.

While absinthe drinking worried many, it wasn't until the drink spread to the working classes that a campaign to ban it spread in many European countries. Public outcry sealed the drink's fate when, in the summer of 1905, a Swiss peasant by the name of Jean Lanfray shot his entire family before turning a rifle upon himself in a botched suicide attempt. Never mind that Lanfray was a serious alcoholic who'd drunk, just the day before killing his family, a crème de menthe, a cognac, six glasses of wine with lunch, a glass of wine before leaving work, a cup of coffee with brandy in it, a liter of wine after getting home. The two glasses of absinthe that he'd drunk before work were surely what led to such an evil act. It was the final nail in the coffin for the herbal drink.

A Fall from Grace

Recent research has shown how absinthe was a political victim—a scapegoat for many social ills of the time—and much has been written on the history of absinthe. Let's just say it started out on a far nobler foot than the vilified drink it was later considered. One story of absinthe's creation has it as the invention of one Dr. Pierre Ordinaire, a French monarchist who fled to Switzerland in the later 1700s. By the time of his death, in 1821, the drink was already called *le Fee Verte*, or the Green Fairy. Other sources tell of the Henriod sisters coming up with the original concoction we call absinthe on their own. Either way, the drink was popular in Switzerland, guaranteeing that production of the drink continued.

In the late 1790s, a Major Dubied discovered absinthe and realized its positive effects on digestion. Absinthe also improved the appetite and helped with fever and chills. Dubied enthusiastically began commercial manufacturing of absinthe, later moving his plant to France to avoid the import fees on an increasingly popular drink. His company, Pernod Fils, is still a major alcohol manufacturer in France, switching to the creation of anise-flavored drinks after the ban on absinthe.

France started expanding its empire into northern Africa in 1830. By the mid-1840s, expansion efforts were at their peak. Malaria and dysentery were rampant problems throughout the army. Someone, having heard of Ordinaire's potent tonic, began giving the troops daily rations of absinthe to help with malaria and other fevers. It also served to kill bacteria in their drinking water and thereby alleviating dysentery. When the victorious troops returned home, they continued enjoying their health-saving drink. French soldiers, enjoying their late afternoon absinthe on a Parisian café terrace, became an image of patriotic pride in which the French middle classes soon joined. The Green Hour was born.

Unfortunately, the enjoyable taste of absinthe, combined with its high alcoholic content, led to the drink being consumed in larger and larger quantities in France and elsewhere.

The drinking of absinthe spread from the retired military, to the upper middle class, to the bohemian and artistic classes, and, finally, to the working class. At each stop along the way, it moved further from a noble drink that saved soldiers' lives and more toward the notorious "Queen of Poisons."

A Word of Caution

Aside from the high alcohol content—the current bottle in our freezer is 136 proof—absinthe does contain thujone, which is present in wormwood, one of the herbs of absinthe. Thujone is a powerful poison that causes extreme convulsions and death. Thujone poisoning leaves the victim unconscious, while violent convulsions set in and increase in severity until they are continuous. Since several of those who died before the ban on absinthe suffered convulsions and seizures toward the very end of their lives, absinthe took the blame for it. In truth, many of these unfortunate folks were true alcoholics who suffered from malnutrition, or even outright starvation. Some also suffered from mental illness that was often caused by syphilis.

The truth of the matter is that you need an awful lot of thujone to cause poisoning. Even those who have never gone near alcohol have ingested thujone, which is present in several other herbs, including sage, hyssop, fennel, and certain mints.

Thujone belongs to a class of chemicals known as terpenes, which are a form of hydrocarbons usually found in essential oils. They are used as solvents and by scientists and nature alike in the synthesis of organic compounds. Terpenes are major components in resins, including turpentine, which is produced from a resin. It's been speculated that Vincent van

Gogh drank turpentine, as well as his paints, because he was addicted to and craved terpenes.

Now, before you panic at the thought of these "poisons" in your herb cabinet, please relax. We need terpenes. They are some of nature's essential biological building blocks. For example, vitamin A is a terpene. It's just that people were looking for something to blame back before the absinthe ban. Once thujone was isolated, and it was realized just how deadly it could be, it became the obvious bad guy. Even when cooler scientific heads called research into question, the court of public opinion had already tried wormwood (and absinthe) and found it guilty.

Pretty much any bottle of absinthe worth drinking contains the following three herbs: wormwood, anise, and fennel. As you'll easily see, all of them have many of the same therapeutic uses. Combined into one tonic, absinthe packed a triple threat for what ailed those of the early nineteenth century (and today).

A Few Words about Wormwood

Wormwood (*Artemisia absinthium*), or grand wormwood, is the plant that not only gives wormwood its name, but which also caused all the controversy. Absinthe, as it's called in France, has a very long history as a medicinal plant. It is mentioned in the Ebers Papyrus as well as in the works of Pythagoras, Hippocrates, Galen, Pliny, and Paracelsus. Dioscorides even suggests it as a remedy for drunkenness, which, given the herb's stimulant properties, isn't nearly as ridiculous and far-fetched as it sounds. Many a drinker of absinthe, including yours truly, has reported a clear-headed effect after having had a drink. Of course, to help place things in perspective, that clear-headedness is often tinged by the high alcohol content of the drink. It's also been suggested in the past that wormwood helps one have visionary dreams, which also doesn't hurt absinthe's notorious reputation.

Above all, wormwood is used for stomach issues such as indigestion, gastric pain, and lack of appetite. Several different herbal sources list it as a tonic, stomachic, carminative, and chologogue. It helps stimulate both the liver and the gallbladder to function better.

Wormwood is also considered an antiseptic and antipyretic. It was these uses that led the French army to include a measure of absinthe daily as part of its troops' rations worldwide after it had proven itself effective with the troops serving in Algeria. Or course, absinthe was also blamed for France's loss to Germany during the Franco-Prussian War, so these things can be a bit subjective.

Further uses of wormwood suggest it can be used as an anthelmintic; the powdered flowering tops expel intestinal worms.

Under carefully supervised use, the oil is said to be a cardiac stimulant, which will improve circulation. Personally, I'd look for other, safer herbs before tempting fate. However, the oil is also good used topically on areas suffering from rheumatism, neuralgia, and arthritis. It works as a local anesthetic.

Wormwood is also a useful herb in the garden, where it makes an excellent companion plant. The roots of wormwood give off a secretion that inhibits the growth of nearby plants, helping with weed control. (I'm wondering if it can help tame mints.) Planted along the edge of a plot, it will also help repel insect larvae. Furthermore, an infusion of the leaves makes a good spray against other pests. They don't like the smell.

Finally, remember that any drink containing wormwood will also need something to help mask the bitterness. Perhaps the only plant with a more bitter taste is rue.

Anise for Flavor

If wormwood gives absinthe its name, anise (*Pimpinella anisum*) gives it flavor. Part of what gives anise its flavor is the chemical compound anethole, a phytoestrogen. The cool part about this is that alcohol is better at extracting the medicinal properties of anise than water. This includes anethole. Furthermore, anethole causes a milky, opaque effect when mixed with even a small amount of water. Part of the beauty of absinthe for many drinkers is the ritual of adding ice cold water to the alcohol very slowly, watching the two liquids swirl around together and combine into one cloudy drink. This is known as louching and is caused by the essential oils in the absinthe leaving their suspension in the alcohol as the water interacts with it. Anethole is a direct contributor to this effect.

Anise is also used primarily for stomachic problems and is used to treat several digestive problems. It helps improve appetite and digestion, relieves flatulence, and can help soothe a colicky baby. It is claimed to help relieve menstrual cramps and nausea. For a simple insomnia cure, allow a few seeds to steep in warm milk and then drink. You should be asleep in no time.

In short, anise is considered an antispasmodic, aromatic, carminative, digestive, stimulant, stomachic, and a tonic. It is considered so useful and flavorful that the anise-flavored drink, pastis, quickly took the place of absinthe after the latter was banned in France. Finally, anise is also the predominant herb in absinthe.

Finally, Fennel

The final herb in our "big three" is Florence fennel (*Foeniculum vulgare*). Fennel also contains anethole, although fennel doesn't have as strong a flavor as anise. Also, in a true connection to debauched drinking, fennel stalks, which are hollow, were the traditional material for the bacchanalian wands of Dionysus and his followers.

Surprise, surprise—fennel is also an excellent stomach herb, helping increase appetite and relieve cramps and flatulence. It's considered a carminative, antispasmodic, aromatic, diuretic, stimulant, and a stomachic. Like anise, a light fennel infusion is good for helping colicky babies. Also like anise, this herb is considered an expectorant.

The oil can be used externally to help ease rheumatoid arthritis pain.

These three herbs—anise, wormwood, and fennel—are found in all absinthe recipes, which is why they're so important. Some recipes just rely on the big three, while others incorporate additional herbs into the initial distillation. Perhaps we should take a quick look at how absinthe is made.

How Absinthe is Made Makes a Difference

The quality of an absinthe depends on the manufacturing methods used to produce it. At the top of the list are the Swiss absinthes. The name refers to the process rather than the country of origin, although several absinthe brands do come from Switzerland. In the Swiss process, herbs and alcohol undergo a heated maceration twice. The first time anise, wormwood, and fennel are added to a quality, high-proof alcohol that's already been distilled. After several hours, water is added and the mixture undergoes distillation. At this point, the manufacturer has a high-proof, very flavorful, clear liquid, but the flavor isn't considered all that stable. That comes with the next step in which additional herbs, such as mint, hyssop, lemon balm, and coriander, are added and the whole lot is allowed to macerate under heat yet again. It's also at this step that absinthe gets its color, thanks to a transfer of chlorophyll from some of the herbs that are added to the alcohol.

"Le bleue," or clear absinthe, is also possible, as are brownish colored ones. It's allowed to cool slowly and then water is added to the mixture once again. The absinthe is passed through a fine sieve to strain out all the herbal bits and pieces. Finally, it's placed into barrels to age. This method yields some truly wonderful tasting absinthes.

Cold-mixed absinthes, which may very well have been what many of the less well-to-do folks drank before the ban, are not macerated or distilled, meaning that they really aren't true absinthes. Flavoring oils and artificial coloring agents are added to a high-proof alcohol and then it is sold as absinthe. Cold-mixed absinthes are often extremely bitter, even after the addition of a necessary sugar cube or two, and serve mainly to get the imbiber very drunk.

Before the ban, and before legislation and bodies to oversee the purity of our food and drink, it was easy to make an inferior alcohol that looked and perhaps even smelled like true absinthe and then pass it off on an unsuspecting public. These drinks were often colored with harsh, poisonous chemicals such as copper and antimony. No wonder people reacted horribly when drinking the stuff.

Additionally, there is a very high-proof alcohol from the Bohemian region of Europe marketed as absinthe. Apparently its main function is to get you drunk quickly. Pete Wells, writing about absinthe in the *New York Times*, recalls tasting some Czech absinth smuggled into the country in a mouthwash bottle by a friend. He said he would have preferred the mouthwash. From everything I've read on the Czech version of the Green Fairy, this is a pretty good description of the taste. However, this is where we get the ritual of the flaming sugar cube that was used to such wonderful effect in the movie *From Hell*.

Finally, there are so-called "absinthe kits" on the market that claim to help you make your own absinthe at home by either adding oils to alcohol or by soaking herbs in it. These "absinthes" are a lot like the cold-mixed ones in both quality and taste. However, some ancient and historic recipes for a wormwood flavored wine are made this way.

How to Serve Absinthe

Drinking absinthe is a matter of personal taste, although it's best ice-cold. Traditionally, because it's a distillate, absinthe is drunk after being mixed with water. There is an entire ritual that goes with this, as the ice-cold water must be slowly added to the alcohol. The usual ratio is 1 part absinthe to 4 or 5 parts water, and there were even special glasses to help you measure it out. The water can be slowly added as is, or you can add to the ritual with the use of an absinthe spoon.

Sometimes a sugar cube was used, especially for the inferior tasting brands. The sugar would be placed on the spoon and then water would be allowed to trickle down over it until it all dissolved into the glass. High-quality absinthes don't need the addition of the sugar, though. And for goodness sake, don't burn it, otherwise all you can taste is burnt sugar.

There are also several absinthe cocktails that have been created over the years. Recipes are floating around on the Internet and can be quite easy to find. A historically favorite drink at the Absinthe House in New Orleans is the absinthe frappe, where the absinthe is poured into a small glass over chipped ice. It's a pretty refreshing drink.

Here in our household, we like our absinthe neat (without anything added). The flavors are very intense, and we drink it in small amounts, since we're all only occasional drinkers. (A liter bottle will last us at least a year.)

Why do we drink absinthe? At first it was to soothe my curiosity over a drink that had long been a fascination of mine. However, we've all come to love the taste, even my husband, who won't go near anything with the flavor of anise or licorice. It's a good drink to sip to relieve congestion or a sore throat. It will settle a too-full tummy, as long as you stick to a small amount. Otherwise, I think the strong alcohol has the opposite effect.

The Ban on Absinthe

By this point you're probably wondering how we can be discussing the drinking of absinthe if the United States banned it back in 1912. Personally, I'd like to thank the Swiss manufacturers of the drink. Many of them never completely stopped producing absinthe, even after it was banned in their country in 1910. At the turn of the twenty-first century, a Swiss distillery by the name of Kubler undertook the job of changing the Swiss constitution to overturn their country's ban on absinthe. Just a few years later, the same task was tried here in the

United States. At about the same time, an American company called Viridian Spirits also started pressuring the Department of the Treasury's Alcohol and Tobacco Tax and Trade Bureau (TTB) to lift the ban on the manufacture and importation of absinthe. Viridian's Lucid Superieure hit the U.S. market just a few weeks before Kubler Swiss Absinthe. The hardest part of the battle was convincing the TTB that absinthe was not an evil word associated with some sort of drug usage. What we drink is considered thujone-free, according to U.S. standards, meaning it contains less than 10 parts per million of thujone. In that regard, the drink is more than safe.

So, if you feel inclined and have fallen under the lure of the Green Fairy, if you want to see if the drink is a tonic as originally claimed, drink up! Please, just make sure you get a good bottle that was made in the Swiss process method so you can truly enjoy your walk with the notorious absinthe.

A quick note if you truly are thinking of buying some absinthe. We purchased our absinthe through the mail from a business called DrinkUpNY. I'm not necessarily endorsing any one supplier. We've just had good luck with them and I'd trust the quality of the absinthe brands they carry. Cheaper usually isn't better in the case of absinthe.

Resources

Baker, Phil. *The Book of Absinthe*. New York, NY: Grove Press, 2001.

Cunningham, Scott. *Cunningham's Encyclopedia of Magical Herbs*. St. Paul, MN: Llewellyn Publications, 1992.

Hutton, Ian. "Thujone: Separating Myth from Reality." Retrieved from The Fee Verte Absinthe House at http://www.feeverte.net/thujone.html.

La Fee Verte. "Fee Verte FAQ." The Fee Verte Absinthe House. http://www.feeverte.net/about.html.

Lust, John. *The Herb Book*. New York, NY: Bantam Books, 1974.

Physicians' Desktop Reference. "Herbal Remedies, Supplements A-Z Index." Thomson Reuters. http://www.pdrhealth.com/drugs/altmed/altmed-a-z.aspx.

Rothstein, Edward. "Absinthe Returns in a Glass Half Full of Mystique and Misery." *The New York Times*. http://www.nytimes.com/2007/11/12/arts/12conn.html?scp=4&sq=absinthe&st=cse.

The Virtual Absinthe Museum. Oxygenee Ltd. http://www.oxygenee.com/absinthe-museum.html.

Wells, Pete. "Liquor of Legend Makes a Comeback." *The New York Times*. Retrieved from http://www.nytimes.com/2007/12/05/dining/05absi.html?scp+8&sq=wabsinthe&st=cse.

Serving Up Summer

by Alice DeVille

When the economy slows or a recession hits, it's only natural to put the focus on your work and stay busy to cope with the tension. Yet during this period, life goes on and you can benefit more from uplifting activities. Summer especially is a vital time for letting go, enjoying seasonal foods and creating celebrations. What better way to recharge your energy than engaging in exciting activities that include warm-weather gatherings in your own back yard? Whether you're preparing treats for family and friends or hosting a party for a crowd, you'll enjoy some simple, inexpensive ways to electrify your summer and make

your outdoor gathering colorful, easy, and fun regardless of economic trends.

This article helps you bring the fun back into your life with tips on party planning, decorating, and delicious food to feed your guests!

Summer Party Checklist

Consider these steps for planning your outdoor party. When the happy day arrives, you'll breeze into it with minimal stress and enjoy the event as much as your guests.

Two to Four Weeks Ahead

- Make a guest list and send out invitations via an e-vite, mail, or phone.

- Plan the menu.

- Decide on a theme and what type of decorations you'll use.

- Create a seating and setup plan for your outdoor event; whether it is a garden, deck, or patio party, you will need adequate chairs and space for tables, and food and beverage stations.

- Arrange to borrow or rent equipment you don't have.

One to Two Weeks Ahead

- Do indoor and outdoor cleaning and yard work, especially time-consuming tasks that you won't be able to accommodate as the party date nears.

- Make a grocery list and shop for menu items, charcoal, or gas canisters.

- Inventory tableware including linens and replace as necessary; order flowers, meat, and seafood.

- Make decorations and centerpieces, string outdoor lighting for a night event, and select music and equipment you need for creating a mood.

Two to Three Days Ahead

- Shop for all but perishable items.

- Clean grill and hose down patio or deck.

- Assemble serving pieces and make labels to present every dish attractively.

- Plan a realistic timetable for cooking and serving food.

One Day Ahead

- Pick up any borrowed items and arrange party layout.

- Shop for last-minute items and perishables.

- Do touch-up cleaning so everything sparkles.

- Pick fresh herbs and vegetables from the garden for use in your planned dishes.

- Prepare as many recipes and gather as many ingredients you'll use as possible; thaw frozen items in refrigerator.

Morning of Party

- Buy ice and fill coolers with drinks and ice.

- Decorate tables and set up serving pieces, plates, and utensils. Don't forget to add herbs to garnish plates and pick flowers for an attractive centerpiece.

- Prepare foods according to your desired timetable.

- Put finishing touches on the meal and table, including setting up receptacles for trash and recyclables.

- Turn on decorative lighting and turn off the sprinkler system and security lights.

- Open wine, light candles, and set out appetizers.

Open-air Entertaining

Have two or three coolers on hand. Put labels on them and plenty of ice inside to keep beverages cool. Designate one for bottled water, another for beer, and a third for diet and regular soft drinks. Consider placing them under shade trees, a covered porch, or a tent if your budget permits. Shade has tremendous entertainment value and gives guests a good reason to take a break from the sun. Two or more food stations will keep guests from congregating in one place and keep the serving line moving more efficiently. Station cups, plates, utensils, napkins, and condiments strategically so guests don't have to get out of line to search for them. Consider using colorful, napkin-lined flower pots in various sizes to hold pretzels, nuts, chips, and sandwich rolls. If you are cooking outdoors, be sure to allow enough time to heat the grill for your veggies, steaks, chicken, and kebobs. A separate dessert station complete with plates and tableware puts a sweet finish to your festive meal. Have an indoor contingency plan ready in case Mother Nature serves up summer rains.

Summer Menu Selections

Have you ever thought about harvesting the foods and flowers you grow to complement the party fare you're serving for your special event? Take inventory of your back yard plot with its succulent tomatoes and squash, deck boxes overflowing with basil, rosemary and thyme, large planters filled with red and yellow peppers, and flower pots brimming with colorful Gerbera daisies, coleus, and fragrant lavender plants ready to dress up your serving table.

Use herbs from your garden or the farmer's market to enhance the flavor of your summer cuisine. Not only will herbs add subtle accents to your main dishes and salads, herbs bring fragrance and interest to favorite dessert and beverage recipes. If you're not using fresh herbs, remember that dried herbs are very potent so reduce the amount you use by half or more. Include your home-grown produce in a salad course, and specimens from your gorgeous summer flower beds in a welcoming table centerpiece.

Tips

- Prepare dishes with components that can be assembled ahead of time yet are savory and crowd pleasing.

- If using a grill, be sure it is the right temperature to prevent scorching on the outside before the food cooks on the inside.

- Brush lean meat with a glaze to add moisture and par-boil potatoes to ensure even cooking.

- Potatoes hold up better in grilled dishes and vegetable packs if you leave the skin on.

Here are two sample menus that make use of fresh herbs and veggies. The recipes include ideas for side and main dishes, sandwiches, breads, desserts, and beverages. Each recipe serves at least 8; double recipe as you desire.

Menu 1

Herbed Corn

Adapted from *Washington Post* food supplement.

Ingredients:

> 6 ears shucked corn
>
> 3 slices uncooked bacon
>
> 4 large shallots, finely chopped (or substitute 1 large red onion)
>
> 2 teaspoons chopped fresh thyme (or 1 teaspoon dried thyme)
>
> 1 teaspoon sea salt
>
> ½ teaspoon freshly ground black pepper
>
> 1½ cups water
>
> ¼ cup heavy cream (optional)
>
> Chopped fresh chives for garnish

Directions:

1. Use a serrated knife to cut the corn kernels off the cobs. Place them in a large bowl, breaking up any connected kernels with your fingers. Use the blade of a utility knife to scrape the cobs into the bowl of corn, releasing the pulp and milky liquid they hold to yield 6 cups.

2. Line a plate with several layers of paper towels.

3. Fry the bacon in a large skillet over medium heat until

crisp and drain on paper towel-lined plate. Crumble.

4. Pour off all but 2 tablespoons of fat from the skillet. Heat over medium heat until oil shimmers; add the shallots, cooking and stirring occasionally for 3 to 4 minutes until lightly golden; while stirring, dislodge any browned bits on the bottom of the skillet.

5. Add the corn, thyme, salt, and pepper to the pan; stir to combine.

6. Add the water and reduce heat to medium low; cook, stirring occasionally, for 30 minutes, until the liquid looks lightly thickened rather than watery.

7. Add the bacon and the cream; increase the heat to medium and cook, stirring as needed, for 5 to 10 minutes until most of the liquid has evaporated.

8. Transfer to a serving bowl and sprinkle with chopped fresh chives. Serve hot.

Grilled Sirloin Salad

Ingredients:

      3 cups Italian salad dressing

      2 pounds beef sirloin steak

      1 pound new potatoes, cut into quarters

      2 10-ounce packages mixed salad greens

      6 tomatoes, chopped

      ½ medium red or purple onion, sliced in thin rings

Directions:

1. Marinate beef in 1 cup of salad dressing for at least 4 hours.

2. Divide potatoes in half and place each half on a double layer of heavy-duty aluminum foil.

3. Cover each with ½ cup salad dressing; fold into packages.

4. Place potatoes and steaks on grill over medium heat and grill 15 minutes, or until meat is cooked (medium) and potatoes are tender.

5. Turn packets occasionally; steaks only once.

6. Cut steaks across grain in thin strips.

7. Toss with potatoes, greens, tomato, onion, and the remaining 1 cup of dressing. (Do not use dressing from marinade.)

Tangerine-Honey Glazed Chicken

Adapted from Bobby Flay, www.parade.com.

Ingredients:

> 3 cups tangerine juice or tangerine-orange juice combo (not from concentrate)
>
> 5 fresh thyme sprigs
>
> ¼ cup honey
>
> Kosher salt and black pepper
>
> 3 tablespoons Spanish paprika
>
> 1 tablespoon ground cumin
>
> 1 tablespoon dry mustard powder
>
> 2 teaspoons ground fennel seeds
>
> 2 tablespoons canola or salad oil
>
> 4 whole boneless chicken breasts, about 8 ounces each (split after cooking)
>
> 2 green onions, thinly sliced, for garnish

Directions:

1. Combine the juice and thyme in a medium saucepan and bring to a boil over high heat. Cook, stirring occasionally, until thickened and reduced to about ½ cup; remove thyme stems and discard.

2. Whisk in the honey until incorporated and season with ½ teaspoon of salt and ¼ teaspoon of pepper. Transfer to a bowl and let cool to room temperature.

3. Stir together the paprika, cumin, mustard powder, fennel, and 1 teaspoon each of the kosher salt and black pepper in a small bowl.

4. Brush both sides of chicken with oil, season with salt and pepper; rub the top of each breast with some of the spice rub and place on grill with the rub-side down over medium-high heat.

5. Cook without touching until they are lightly golden brown and a crust has formed, 3 to 4 minutes. Turn breasts over, brush tops liberally with some of the glaze, flip them, and continue cooking until thermometer inserted into the center registers 155°F.

6. Remove from grill, brush the spice-rub side with more glaze, tent loosely with foil and let rest 5 minutes before cutting in half and serving.

Herbed Corn Bread

Ingredients:

> 1½ cups self-rising cornmeal
>
> ¾ cup self-rising flour
>
> 1 teaspoon sugar

½ teaspoon dried or 1 teaspoon fresh marjoram

½ teaspoon dried or 1 teaspoon fresh thyme

¼ teaspoon celery seed

2 eggs, beaten

1¼ cups milk

6 tablespoons butter, melted

Directions:

1. Preheat oven to 425°F. Lightly grease 9-inch square pan.

2. Combine dry ingredients in a large bowl.

3. Combine eggs, milk, and butter. Add to dry ingredients, stirring until just moistened.

4. Pour into pan and bake for 25 minutes or until golden brown.

Rosemary Orange Mini Cupcakes

Ingredients for cakes:

1 package yellow cake mix

1 3.4-ounce package instant lemon pudding mix

4 eggs

¾ cup cold water

¼ cup vegetable oil

1 teaspoon finely crushed fresh rosemary

Ingredients for glaze:

3 cups confectioners' sugar

½ cup frozen orange juice concentrate, thawed

3 tablespoons melted butter

3 tablespoons water

Directions:

1. Preheat oven to 325°F. Grease two miniature muffin pans.

2. In mixing bowl, combine the cake mix, pudding mix, eggs, water, and oil, and beat well.

3. Fill the prepared muffin pans using about 1 tablespoon batter for each cake.

4. Bake for 10-12 minutes, or until the cakes spring back when touched.

5. Prepare the glaze by mixing the confectioners' sugar, orange juice, butter, and water until smooth; set aside.

6. Dip the mini cupcakes in the glaze immediately after removing them from the oven.

7. Drain on waxed paper. Repeat process until you use all the batter. Makes 7 to 8 dozen bite-size treats.

Plantation Iced Tea

(From Paula Deen, adapted from Southern recipe)

Ingredients:

>7 tea bags
>
>12 mint leaves
>
>½ cup sugar
>
>1 6-ounce can frozen lemonade concentrate
>
>1 12-ounce can pineapple juice

Directions:

1. Pour 4 cups boiling water over the tea bags, mint, and sugar in a large pitcher. Steep for 30 minutes.

2. Remove the tea bags, squeezing out excess liquid.

3. Remove the mint.

4. Prepare the lemonade according to instructions and add to the tea.

5. Add the pineapple juice and stir well. Pour over ice.

Double recipe as needed. Makes 2 quarts.

Menu II

Mustard Grilled Salmon Salad

Ingredients:

> 2 pounds salmon fillet, cut into 8 pieces
>
> 4 red bell peppers, sliced
>
> 2 zucchini, sliced
>
> 2 yellow summer squash, sliced
>
> 4 cups rotini or fusili pasta
>
> 6 cups mixed salad greens
>
> 2 tablespoons chopped fresh dill for garnish
>
> 2 cups bottled honey mustard dressing

Directions:

1. Brush salmon with 4 tablespoons salad dressing and place on grill.

2. Toss peppers, zucchini, and squash with 2 tablespoons salad dressing and place in a grill basket.

3. Cover and grill 4 to 6 inches from medium heat for 10 to 15 minutes, shaking basket often and turning salmon once. Vegetables should be tender-crisp and salmon should flake easily with fork.

4. Meanwhile, cook and drain pasta according to package directions.

5. Mix with ½ cup dressing.

6. Add cooked vegetables and toss to coat.

7. Arrange greens on 8 plates, top with pasta mixture, then salmon.

8. Drizzle with remaining dressing and sprinkle with dill.

Fresh Herb Potato Salad

Ingredients:

> 4 tablespoons old style mustard (sharp or Dijon tart)
>
> 3 tablespoons olive oil
>
> 2 tablespoons red wine vinegar
>
> 2 tablespoons each freshly chopped flat leaf parsley and chives
>
> 2 pounds cooked, small redskin potatoes, halved or quartered
>
> Salt and pepper to taste

Directions:

1. Whisk together mustard, olive oil, herbs, and red wine vinegar.

2. Add potatoes and sir until completely coated with dressing.

3. Add salt and pepper to taste.

Grilled Chicken Club Sandwiches

Ingredients:

    ¼ cup Dijon mustard

    8 slices country style bread, toasted

    8 thick slices tomato

    8 thick slices cooked bacon

    8 slices grilled chicken breast

    1 cup arugula leaves

    8 slices fresh mozzarella

    Cracked black pepper

    4 basil leaves, thinly sliced

Directions:

1. Spread mustard on each bread slice.

2. Layer 4 slices with 2 slices tomato, 2 bacon strips, 2 slices chicken breast, ¼ cup of arugula leaves, and two slices mozzarella.

3. Season to taste with salt and pepper; top with ribbons of basil and remaining toasted bread.

4. Cut in half, assemble on platter, and serve.

Herb Garlic Sourdough Bread

Ingredients:

    1 large loaf sourdough bread

    Olive oil

    Garlic salt

    Fines herbes from gourmet grocer (or make your own from dried herbs: equal parts parsley, chervil, chives, and tarragon; mix well)

Directions:

1. Preheat the oven to 350°F.

2. Place bread slices on one or two baking sheets.

3. With a pastry brush, brush each slice of bread with olive oil. Sprinkle with garlic salt and a generous sprinkling of *fines herbes*.

4. Bake for 10 minutes, or until the bread begins to brown.

3. Serve in large baskets in the center of each table.

Shortbread Peach Tart

Make this versatile dessert a day before your party to save time.

Ingredients:

Crust

1¼ cups all-purpose flour

½ cup (1 stick) butter, softened

2 tablespoons sour cream

1 teaspoon finely chopped rosemary leaves

Filling

6 or 7 medium peaches, peeled and sliced

3 large egg yolks

¾ cup sour cream

¾ cup sugar

¼ cup all-purpose flour

Grated zest from one lemon

Glaze

½ cup peach preserves or peach jelly

1 tablespoon frozen lemonade concentrate

Directions:

Preheat oven to 375°F.

1. Make crust by placing the flour, butter, sour cream, and rosemary in a food processor and pulse to combine.

2. When dough forms a ball, pat with lightly floured hands into the bottom and sides of an ungreased 10-inch tart pan with a removable bottom and ½-inch sides.

3. Bake for about 15 minutes, until the crust is set but not browned. Let cool while preparing the filling. Lower the oven temperature to 350°F.

2. Make filling by peeling and thickly slicing the peaches. Arrange the fresh peach slices in overlapping circles on top of the crust until it is completely covered. Overfill the crust; peaches will shrink up during cooking.

3. Combine the egg yolks, sour cream, sugar, and flour and beat until smooth. Pour mixture over the peaches.

4. Place the tart pan on a baking sheet and bake for about 1 hour, until the custard sets and is pale golden in color. Cover with an aluminum foil tent or protective grids if the crust starts browning too quickly.

5. Transfer the tart pan to a wire rack to cool. When cool, remove the side wall of the pan.

The glaze:

1. Combine the preserves or jelly with lemonade.

2. Spread with a pastry brush over the top of the warm tart.

Serve the tart warm, at room temperature, or chilled.

Easy Summer Fruit Punch

Make this recipe the day before your party.

Ingredients:

       2 6-ounce cans frozen orange juice concentrate

       2 6-ounce cans frozen lemonade concentrate

       1 48-ounce can pineapple juice

       3 cups sugar

       3 cups water

       2 pints strawberries, hulled

       1 2-liter bottle of Sprite or 7-Up

       Mint sprigs for garnish

Directions:

1. Combine the orange juice, lemonade, and pineapple juice and stir well.

2. Bring 3 cups water and the sugar to a boil in a heavy saucepan, and boil until the sugar is dissolved, about 5 minutes. Let cool.

3. Add the syrup to the fruit juices.

4. Place the whole strawberries into a ring mold that will float in your punch bowl. Pour in enough fruit juice to fill the mold. Freeze.

5. Refrigerate the remaining juice in easy-pour container.

6. When ready to serve, pour the refrigerated fruit juice into a punch bowl and add the Sprite or 7-Up. Float the strawberry ice ring in the punch. Add mint sprigs to center of ring to garnish. Makes 1 gallon of punch.

Note that the baked desserts for each menu call for finely crushed rosemary leaves. If you have cooked with rosemary, a very strong herb, you may think it could be a bit overpowering but surprisingly it is not. Using rosemary in a flour-based crust, cookies, or cake tames the savory quality of this herb. Baked goods bring out the milder side of versatile rosemary.

Asparagus: The Gilded Lady

by Anne Sala

From our first taste thousands of years ago, the human race has been smitten with asparagus. No other vegetable in history appears to have had so much fastidious attention showered upon it by so many different cultures. Yet, few recipes seem capable of improving on its natural flavor, in my opinion.

Asparagus is thought to be native to lands near the Mediterranean Sea. Its name comes from the Persian *asparag*, which means "sprout." It grows best in sandy soil, where the spears can easily push up from its rhizome root system in early spring. Green asparagus is the most commonly grown variety, but it also comes in purple.

The speed at which it grows is one of the reasons asparagus is considered a delicacy. They taste the most vibrantly grassy and green when they are small, so they must be picked very soon after they appear. The bigger they get, the woodier the stalks become.

A member of the lily family (*Lilliaceae*), asparagus shares few characteristics with its other culinary cousins, namely onions, garlic, and leeks. The most significant difference is the way people regard it. While onions and garlic form the backbone of many recipes, they are usually relegated to supporting roles in the dish. *Asparagus officinalis*, on the other hand, is nicknamed the "king of vegetables." We throw celebrations to welcome its arrival after the snows melt and argue over the merits of thin spears versus thick.

Medicinally, asparagus has been used as a diuretic since prehistoric times, but we've been going crazy for it as a vegetable for nearly as long. The Romans regarded asparagus so highly that they froze some of the harvest in the snowy peaks of the Alps so they could enjoy it later, out of season. In the seventeenth century, King Louis XIV of France had state-of-the-art greenhouses built so he could eat asparagus fresh all year round.

As its popularity grew throughout the Western Hemisphere, eating the spears became an even fussier affair. Farmers learned to grow green asparagus without light so the stalks would remain a moonish white—a delicacy's delicacy! Furthermore, the rich ate them using small silver tongs, and served them in special napkins or on platters depicting the stalks neatly tied in string.

While I leave it optional how one decides to present the asparagus at the dinner table, I have attempted to contrast simple ways to serve asparagus alongside more involved preparations. Both types combine its unique flavor with some of its favorite companions: cheese, eggs, and piquant soy sauce.

Guidelines for Choosing Asparagus

Choose asparagus that looks as fresh as possible. The spears should not be limp and the scales of the head should be compact. The woody ends should not be shriveled. The thickness of the stalks cannot be used to determine if one asparagus is better than another. Thick stalks usually mean that particular spear grew from a location closer to the center of the rhizome. Thinner stalks usually grow near the edges of the root system. Choose the thickness of the stalk based on how you plan to prepare it.

Some people peel asparagus, but I do not. To remove the woody end of the stem (if it is thick enough to have a woody end), bend each asparagus until it snaps. Or, cut with a sharp knife. Use the stems to flavor asparagus broth. You can do that immediately or freeze the stems for later.

Steamed Asparagus

Apparently, Emperor Julius Caesar preferred his asparagus with melted butter. This recipe is best when you know the asparagus you have is as fresh as possible. Serves 2 to 4.

> 1 pound asparagus, rinsed
>
> 1 teaspoon salt
>
> Garnishes*

Directions:
1. Remove the woody ends of the asparagus.
2. Fill a sauté pan with water until it reaches 1½ inches and add the salt. Bring it to boil over high heat.

3. Add the asparagus and cover with the lid. Lower the heat and simmer 4 to 6 minutes, depending on the thickness of the asparagus, until a stalk can easily be pierced with a sharp knife.

4. Drain the asparagus and arrange on a serving platter.

5. Garnish with your choice of toppings (salt and pepper, melted butter, olive oil, fresh lemon juice, balsamic vinegar, grated Parmesan cheese, or chopped prosciutto).

Scrambled Eggs with Asparagus

Creamy eggs are one of the best foils for the fresh taste of asparagus. This particular recipe is just as appropriate to serve for supper as it is for breakfast. Serves 2.

> ½ pound asparagus, rinsed
>
> 3 eggs
>
> 2 tablespoons milk
>
> ¼ cup shredded Parmesan cheese
>
> 1 tablespoon unsalted butter
>
> Salt and pepper to taste

Directions:

1. Break off the woody ends of the asparagus.

2. Break eggs into a bowl, add milk, and beat until combined.

3. Melt butter in a medium-sized skillet over medium heat.

4. Pour the egg mixture into the skillet. Once it begins to set, add the asparagus and stir slowly with a wooden spoon until the eggs reach the desired consistency and the asparagus is bright green.

5. Sprinkle with the Parmesan cheese, salt, and pepper, and serve.

Cream of Asparagus Soup

This recipe looks like it has a lot of steps, but that's only because I include the steps needed to make the asparagus broth. If you want to skip that part, and just use water and chicken broth, the soup will retain its refreshingly green flavor. The tarragon in the cream adds a hint of sweetness that makes this a rather elegant soup. Serves 4 to 6.

> 1 pound asparagus, rinsed
>
> 2 cups chicken broth
>
> 3 cups water
>
> 1 cup cream or half-and-half
>
> 4 sprigs fresh tarragon, or ¼ cup dried placed in a metal teaball
>
> 2 medium-size leeks, about 6 cups, rinsed and chopped
>
> 1 cup onion, chopped
>
> 1 tablespoon olive oil

Directions:

1. Pour chicken broth and water into a stock pot and place over medium heat.

2. Break off the woody ends of the asparagus and add to the stock. (You could also add any reserved asparagus ends from previous preparations. The more asparagus in the broth, the more pronounced the flavor.) Raise the heat to high and bring to a boil. Then, lower the heat so the broth simmers for 20 to 45 minutes.

3. Place cream in a small saucepan over medium-low heat. Stir occasionally until small bubbles appear along the edges of the pan.

4. Remove the cream from the heat, add tarragon, and cover. Let steep until ready to use.

5. Chop the remaining asparagus into 1-inch pieces. Set aside.

6. Place a large skillet over medium heat, and add the olive oil.

7. When the oil begins to ripple from the heat, add the onion and leeks. Sauté until soft, at least five minutes.

8. Once the broth has finished simmering, carefully strain the liquid into a second pot, discarding the woody ends. Reserve the first pot to use again later.

9. Bring the broth to a boil again over high heat. Add the asparagus, leeks, and onion. Return to a boil, and then reduce the heat so the soup simmers for 20 minutes.

10. Remove the soup from the heat and allow to cool slightly. Carefully transfer small batches of the soup to a blender or food processor and blend until creamy. Return the blended soup to the first pot.

11. When all the soup is back in the first pot, discard the tarragon from the cream. Gently stir the cream into the soup. Garnish with salt and pepper.

Roasted Sesame Asparagus

While it is true that almost anything tastes good when given a crunchy coating and a side of dipping sauce, the green taste of the asparagus holds its own against the accompanying sharp flavor. Feel free to adjust the ratios of the sauce's ingredients to suit your own tastes. Serves 4 to 6.

> 1 pound asparagus, rinsed
>
> 1 egg white
>
> 1 tablespoon milk
>
> ¼ cup roasted black sesame seeds
>
> ½ cup fine bread crumbs
>
> ⅓ cup soy sauce
>
> 1 tablespoon rice wine vinegar
>
> 1 teaspoon fresh ginger, grated
>
> 1 teaspoon chives, snipped fine
>
> 2 teaspoons sesame oil
>
> 1 teaspoon hot sauce

Directions:

1. Line a cookie sheet with aluminum foil.

2. Break off the woody ends of the asparagus. Dry the spears with paper towels.

3. Place the egg white and milk in shallow bowl. Beat with fork until blended.

4. Mix sesame seeds and bread crumbs in another shallow bowl.

5. Dip each asparagus spear into the egg mixture and then lay it on the breading. Use your fingers to help coat the spear on all sides. Then, place the spear on the prepared cookie sheet.

6. Preheat oven to 375°F.

7. Let coated asparagus rest for 10 minutes.

8. Roast asparagus for at least 10 minutes.

9. Combine the remaining ingredients in a bowl.

The asparagus can be eaten hot or cold. Serve the sauce alongside.

Asparagus Custard with Truffle

This recipe is for when asparagus by itself just isn't decadent enough. If you don't have any truffle products, its omission won't harm the final dish. Consider adding cheese or sautéed regular mushrooms instead. Serves 2.

> ½ pound asparagus, rinsed
>
> 3 eggs, beaten
>
> ¾ cup heavy cream or half-and-half
>
> ½ teaspoon dried onion flakes
>
> ⅓ cup bread crumbs
>
> 1 tablespoon butter
>
> ⅛ teaspoon truffle salt, oil, or grated fresh
>
> ¼ teaspoon cooking salt
>
> Pepper to taste

Directions:

1. Preheat oven to 325°F.

2. Combine dried onion, truffle seasoning, eggs, and cream in a measuring cup with a spout. This way, the onion will soften, and the liquid will be imbued with the flavors while you assemble the rest of the ingredients.

3. Remove the woody ends of the asparagus.

4. Chop the asparagus into ½-inch chunks.

5. Fill a sauté pan with 1½ inches of water and add the salt. Bring to boil over high heat.

6. Cook the asparagus in the boiling water for 2 to 3 minutes. Drain.

7. Divide the asparagus and bread crumbs between two oven-proof ramekins, cups, or bowls (or, use one bowl that is big enough to hold it all).

8. Open the oven door. With oven mitts on, pull out the top rack as far as it can safely go. Set a large oven-proof skillet or roasting pan on it. Place the ramekins in the pan. Carefully and evenly pour the egg mixture into the ramekins. Place dabs of butter on top.

9. Carefully pour hot water into the pan until the level of the water is as high as the level of egg mixture.

10. Gently push the rack back into the oven and allow the custards to bake until a knife inserted into the center comes out clean—at least 20 minutes.

11. Carefully remove the ramekins from the water bath and garnish with pepper. Serve immediately.

Asparagus Risotto

This is the only recipe where I specify the thickness of the asparagus. I think thin spears melt into the risotto in a more appealing fashion than the thicker ones, but the taste will be the same no matter what size is used. Serves 4 to 6.

> 1 pound thin asparagus, rinsed
>
> 3½ to 4 cups asparagus broth (see recipe above)
>
> 2 tablespoons unsalted butter
>
> 1 tablespoon olive oil

1 cup onion, diced

1 cup Arborio rice

¼ cup white wine

½ cup grated Parmesan cheese

Salt and pepper to taste

Directions:

1. Chop the asparagus into small pieces, but keep the tips intact. Chop the rest into pieces about ¼-inch long or smaller.
2. Heat broth and keep it on a nearby burner over low heat.
3. Place a large saucepan over medium heat. Add olive oil and butter.
4. When the butter has melted and foamed, add the onion. Cook until soft, about 6 or 7 minutes.
5. Add rice to the pan. Stir to coat.
6. When the rice is beginning to turn translucent, pour in the wine. Stir until all the wine has been absorbed.
7. With a ladle, pour in about ½ cup of broth. Stir the rice until the broth is absorbed.
8. Continue to stir and use a ladle to occasionally add broth, allowing the rice to absorb almost all of it before adding more.
9. After about 10 minutes, add the asparagus. Continue stirring and adding broth.
10. Cook for 10 to 15 minutes more, until all the broth has been added and the rice is cooked through.
11. Remove the pan from the heat and stir in the cheese. Add salt and pepper to taste. Serve immediately.

Better Butters

⪼ by Harmony Usher ⪻

No one really knows when butter was first made, but we do know it emerged in many cultures around the world as people began keeping milk-producing animals for their own use. Depending on the region, the first butters could have been made from the milk of goats, yaks, buffalo, sheep, or cows. It's quite possible butter was accidentally created when milk was carried over a long distance in a warm container; the gentle agitation causing the separation of milk into butterfat, water, and milk proteins. Today, butter continues to be made around the world from the milk of these same animals, although in North America, the most butter is made from the mild milk from cows and goats. One thing is for sure, though: we have been creating new ways to enhance its creamy goodness since its discovery.

Although butter lost favor for a time when margarine was introduced, it is enjoying a resurgence in popularity. Many people want to use simple "farm foods" of the past, and butter is one such food. With that resurgence is renewed interest in combining butter with herbs, spices, and other ingredients to compliment meats, fish, vegetables, pastas, and baked goods.

Preparation and Storage

Butters with added ingredients are called "compound" or "composite" butters. These can be created in two ways—by pressing additional ingredients into softened butter or by whipping ingredients with a whisk or electric mixer.

Pressed Method

To create a compound butter the pressed way, allow butter to soften to room temperature. Using a good sharp knife, chop or puree the herbs you wish to add. Using a wooden spoon or stiff spatula, press the ingredients into the butter until evenly distributed. Chopped herbs will remain intact and give the butter a speckled appearance, while a pureed herb will give your butter a more even color.

Compound butters made using this method will retain the consistency of butter and keep as long as a simple butter will keep. Hand-mixed compound butters can be scooped into sealable containers and stored in the refrigerator for up to two months, or in the freezer for up to six months.

You can also form the finished butter into a log and wrap it in wax paper and plastic wrap for storing in the freezer.

Storing the compound butter in this way allows you to cut slices—little patties—as you need them. This is a particularly nice way to store these butters if they are going to be used to top hot dishes such as meat or vegetables, where they slowly melt.

Whipped Method

A whipped butter is made by using an electric hand mixer or a whip. Begin by cutting the butter into small squares and allowing it to soften to room temperature. Place chopped or pureed herbs into the butter and whip until light and fluffy. Because this method adds air to the butter, it's consistency will be lighter than butter prepared with the pressed method. Whipped butters will not keep as long as pressed butter, and will melt more quickly and lose their shape in warmer rooms. For these reasons, make them in small batches and close to the time you wish to use them.

There is no hard and fast rule about the ratio of herbs and other ingredients in herb butters. I suggest beginning with ¼ cup of lightly packed herbs to one cup of butter, and adding or reducing the herbs depending on your taste. If you are using a pureed herb, use less, as too much will make your butter too wet to keep its shape. Depending on how you are going to serve the butter, this may be important.

Presentation

Whereas regular butter is typically served in a covered butter dish, compound butters are so pretty you will want everyone to see them! Choose from a variety of presentations suited to either pressed or whipped butter.

Butter Molds

Try serving butter formed into whimsical shapes. You may purchase specially designed butter molds or use candy molds you already have. For single servings, use molds that are approximately one to two teaspoons in size. To use, scoop the prepared butter into the molds and flatten well with a small spatula or knife, making sure to fill the mold completely. Cover with plastic wrap to prevent any unwelcome freezer odor from entering the butter, and freeze. Then pop the butter out of the molds when you are ready to use it.

These can be served on individual plates alongside food, or you can place them in a small bowl or on a platter where people can serve themselves. Shapes such as rose buds, stars, bumblebees, and leaves are pretty, and seasonal shapes are also fun.

If you don't have any molds that would serve this purpose, you can use a melon baller. Gently scoop out little balls of butter and present them in a small dish. You can also purchase larger molds to use when you want to present the butter on a small plate to pass around the table.

Piped Butters

Whipped butter is too light to be used in a mold, but is perfect for piping! Use a standard piping bag (the kind you use for cake decorating) and fill the bag with herb butter. Line a cookie tray with parchment paper, and pipe out little florets, using 1 to 2 teaspoons of butter per serving. Flash freeze the florets for fifteen minutes. Remove them from the parchment paper with a spatula and store in a sealed container.

If the butter is going to be used right away and it is going to be spread on a cold food, you might pipe it directly into a small butter crock or butter dish, which come in individual serving sizes as well as the standard shared size. These butters will melt more quickly than pressed butter so it's important to serve them at, or close to, the time of serving.

Herbal Choices

If you think of herb butters and only envision garlic butter, think again! There is simply no limit to the combinations of herbs you can use. Your choices are limited only by availability and imagination. Much will depend on the food you wish to serve it with. I think of food in categories such as vegetables, meats, fish, and pastas, which helps me decide what herbs I want to use. Generally speaking, stronger tasting foods pair well with stronger flavored herb butters. More delicate dishes such as fish and other seafood welcome subtler flavors.

Vegetables invite the use of basil, oregano, parsley, marjoram, and thyme, which can be joined in any combination. Garlic, of course, is an essential compliment to any of those, as are scapes (the young green tops of the garlic plants), scallions, and green onions. These combinations are particularly good piped onto a baked potato, or worked into mashed potatoes.

If you want a citrus flavor, use herbs such as lemon verbena or lemon balm. Lemon or lime zest and a bit of fresh pressed lemon or lime juice can be added to the butter as well. This is wonderful served on sautéed summer vegetables such as zucchini, red and yellow peppers, and beans.

Meats can be topped with a pat of herb butter when served hot. The effect of watching the butter slowly melting and drizzling over the dish is an elixir for the appetite! Many gourmet chefs are now creating compound butters that have wine or stock reductions worked into them. Herbs can also be combined with fresh citrus juice or hard cheese, such as Parmesan, for mouth-watering variations. If you begin experimenting with spices—cumin, cardamom, nutmeg, cinnamon, etc.—your imagination can run wild. For instance, you might try an Asiago and cracked black pepper butter for your baked potatoes, or a chili pepper and cilantro combination to spice up your fish dishes.

Ending on a Sweet Note

Though we typically think of savory ways to enjoy compound butters, there are endless possibilities for those among you who love butter on muffins, quick loaves, pancakes, and waffles. Sweet butters typically make use of the citrus and licorice flavored herbs, which are wonderful combined with small amounts of icing sugar, lemon or lime zest, or edible flower petals. Imagine a butter made with a combination of lemon balm, fresh raspberries, and a little confectioners' sugar. How about a butter made with the addition of candied ginger and lime? Now imagine either of these spread on your favorite fresh-baked tea biscuit or scone—mmmm! When adding honey, melted chocolate, or maple syrup to butter, the butter will have a softer consistency and is not likely to lend itself to being formed into shapes. No worries—simply serve in a little bowl with a spoon or spreader and guests can dollop it on!

Herbs that Love Butter

Basil
Parsley
Oregano
Marjoram
Thyme
Tarragon
Garlic
Garlic scapes
Cilantro
Lemon balm
Lemon verbena
Anise
Ginger root
Cracked black pepper

Complimentary Savory Ingredients

Asiago cheese
Parmesan cheese
Anchovies
Capers

Complimentary Sweet Ingredients

Lemon, lime, and orange juice
Vanilla
Nutmeg
Allspice
Cinnamon
Confectioners' sugar
Cocoa powder
Citrus zest

Ground nuts such as almond, walnut, and hazelnut
Natural extracts such as banana, lemon, and almond
Honey
Maple syrup

Herbs
for
Health
and
Beauty

Heady Herbs

❧ by Dallas Jennifer Cobb ❧

D o you ever wish you had a
secret stash of some instant
cure for all that ails you?
Have you ever wondered if maybe
there were a few herbs that could aid
you and your loved ones, herbs with
widespread properties and healing
powers, a couple of herbs to keep
around the house, as a first aid kit of
sorts?

Well, when it comes to ailments
of the head, there are a few herbs with
healing properties that you should
know about. These herbs are good for
a variety of ailments, including headache, poor memory, lack of mental
clarity, and focus. There are herbs that
can help with common kids' ailments

from a mild case of restlessness to the more debilitating attention-deficit hyperactivity disorder (ADHD); and herbs that can help the elderly with common ailments from mild forgetfulness to debilitating Alzheimer's. These "heady herbs" help to decrease stress-induced symptoms, increase circulation and blood flow to the brain, and contribute to calming neurological disorders.

With increased access to information about ailments through the Internet and a variety of digital tools, people have greater access to definitions of ailments, and ideas on how to cope with or remedy complaints for a wide variety of neurological disorders. Whether new communication technology has increased our awareness or whether medical diagnosis has improved, both are contributing to an increase in the number of people with a confirmed neurological condition, impairment, or ailment.

People are interested in information that can help them tackle their minor ailments head-on, whether it is stress, sleep disorders, or ailments. This article lists some of the heady herbs that are known to help alleviate symptoms that may be bothering you.

While the information in this article is intended to inform and educate, please remember that herbs should never be used casually. Herbs are very powerful. Always seek the help of a qualified and experienced herbalist, who can recommend herbs appropriate to your symptoms and suggest specific therapeutic amounts, frequency, and uses.

Headaches and Migraines

A headache is any minor ache of the head that does not frequently recur, does not persist for several days, is not caused by a blow to the head or a fall, and does not involve a loss of consciousness. These are far more serious symptoms that could indicate something other than a headache, and you should consult a doctor if you have such symptoms.

Minor headaches can be triggered by a variety of causes, including a cold, sinus blockage, eyestrain, stress, muscular tension, hunger, low blood sugar from not eating, dehydration, dilation of the blood vessels in the head and scalp, hormonal imbalance, premenstrual syndrome, food sensitivities, or medication. Tension headaches are a result of tight muscles in the neck and head, and usually occur as a result of anger, fear, stress, depression, or anxiety. The brain itself does not feel pain, so headaches stem from tissues in the head, neck, scalp, and the covering of the brain.

A migraine is a more serious sort of headache that is associated with vascular constriction and dilation, and may involve a disturbance of the serotonin metabolism, causing dilation of cerebral arteries followed by vascular spasms of the cranial blood vessels. Migraines may appear in childhood, but more commonly start in late teens or early twenties. They are more common to women than men and frequently end with menopause.

Migraine pain usually begins on one side of the head, and takes many hours to develop. It can spread to the entire head, last for several days, and be accompanied by nausea, sensitivity to light and noise, and intense pain.

Migraines can be recognized by their early warning signs, called "aura." These signs include a minor loss of vision, feeling strange or dissociated, seeing flashing lights, and even feeling a burning, twitching, or weakness in the muscles. Many migraine sufferers find that if they take a remedy or medicine when they first feel the aura, they can stave off a full-blown migraine attack.

Herbs for Headaches and Migraines

Butterbur

Butterbur (*Petasites hybridus*) is commonly recommended for use as both a treatment for and a preventive of headaches and migraines. With anti-spasmodic and anti-inflammatory qualities, butterbur can reduce muscle tension and calm the spasm of blood vessels that is a symptom of severe headaches. Butterbur is often combined with feverfew.

Cayenne Pepper

Cayenne pepper (*Capsicum annuum*) contains capsaicin, which helps to relieve pain. Used in the form of a nasal spray, it is useful in the treatment of headaches. Eating peppers of any sort causes the stomach to send messages to the brain, stimulating the production of endorphins that make the body feel good and are a natural painkiller.

Chamomile and Valerian

Chamomile (*Chamaemelum nobile*) promotes relaxation, and valerian (*Valeriana officinalis*), which is a natural sedative, supports healthy neurotransmitter balances, relieves stress symptoms, and promotes sleep.

Feverfew

Feverfew (*Tanacetum parthenium*) is most often recommended as a daily supplement suitable for preventing migraines. It can inhibit the clumping of platelets and regulate the release of serotonin from the blood vessels, producing stable serotonin levels and reduced vascular constrictions. The overall effect is a reduction in both the number and the severity of migraines.

Ginko

Ginko (*Ginko biloba*) improves the flow of blood to the brain, carrying oxygen. Increased oxygen can relieve headaches, and improve memory and alertness. Because gingko can produce side effects when taken with common medications, always seek qualified advice before taking it.

Passionflower

Passionflower (*Passiflora alata*) can help you to sleep, calms the nerves, and lowers anxiety. It also possesses anti-inflammatory qualities and is a known painkiller.

Recipe for Migraine Tea

A widely used recipe for Migraine Tea is listed in the July 1995 issue of *Mother Earth News*. The recipe is frequently referred to by herbalists and enthusiasts as a reliable treatment and prevention tea for migraine sufferers. Containing a number of beneficial herbs, it is also good-tasting and aromatic.

Combine:

> 6 parts rosemary leaves
>
> 4 parts peppermint leaves
>
> 4 parts lemon balm leaves

4 parts sweet violet leaves

3 parts feverfew

½ part sweet violet flowers

Directions:

Mix thoroughly and store in a glass container, away from bright light and moisture. When you need it, measure a tablespoon into a mug and steep in hot water for 5 minutes before drinking.

The addition of rosemary (*Rosmarinus officinalis*) means this tea promotes vasodilation and peripheral blood flow. Because it also stimulates and refreshes, it is a good daily tea to take for migraine prevention.

Memory Problems

My grandfather loved to tell this joke at every family gathering. "I've been losing my memory," he'd say. "I got some gingko, because it's supposed to help stimulate my memory, but I keep forgetting to take it."

Whether you have mild forgetfulness, sometimes feel overwhelmed with information, or suffer more severe memory problems like Alzheimer's, there are herbs that can help. The differences between memory problems and Alzheimer's are significant. If you forget what you did this morning, you have a memory problem. It could be a result of stress, feeling overwhelmed, or exhaustion. Alzheimer's is characterized by the forgetting of things that you have known all your life. Alzheimer's causes people to forget concepts like red means stop or hot stoves burn hands. It is the forgetting of concepts crucial to safety and survival that makes progressed Alzheimer's so dangerous.

Whether you ascribe to the filing cabinet theory of memory (our minds are like big filing cabinets, and the longer we live, the more files there are to search through to find what we want), or the automobile theory (our minds are like car engines, and the valves and gaskets get worn and loose over time), we can all agree that as we age, our memory ages, too. Often the best stimulants to memory are oxygen from light exercise and improved circulation, good nutrition, good sleep habits, and joyous living. Before you reach for a herbal remedy, why not try some positive lifestyle changes first and see if they can help. If you still need help, try the following.

Memory Stimulants

Herbs can help memory by stimulating blood circulation to the brain, relaxing blood vessels, and preventing the chance of stroke, which is another major cause of memory loss.

For short-term memory stimulation, there is nothing like caffeine to help give you a boost. Researchers at the Medical University Innsbruck in Austria have demonstrated that caffeine boosts short-term working memory. "We were able to show that caffeine modulates a higher brain function through its effects on distinct areas of the brain."[1]

The most popular herbs to remedy memory loss are gingko biloba, rosemary, ginseng, and green tea. These herbs appear to stimulate blood flow, carry oxygen to the brain, and

1. Tudor, Raiciu. "Caffeine Boosts Short-Time Memory." World and Health News at http://news.softpedia.com/news/Caffeine-Boosts-Short-Time-Memory-13828.shtml (accessed September 6, 2009.)

prevent cholesterol from turning into plaque. That means they reduce the risk of stroke by limiting the amount of plaque that is deposited, and hardens, in the arteries.

Dandelion

Dandelion (*Taraxacum officinale*) promotes healthy brain cell function through superior nutrition. Dandelion contains high levels of vitamins A and C, and is a natural source of lecithin, which is known to elevate the brain's level of acetylcholine and play a role in stemming Alzheimer's disease.

Gingko

Gingko (*Gingko biloba*) contains high amounts of antioxidants, which counteract the effects of cellular aging, and boost the immune system. Gingko also stimulates blood circulation, enhancing the flow of blood and oxygen to the brain.

Ginseng

Ginseng is widely reputed to be a memory stimulant and an energy booster, increasing blood circulation to the brain. There are several kinds of ginseng, but the most potent and effective for memory stimulation are the Asian (*Panax ginseng*) and American (*Panax quinquefolius*) varieties. Both belong to the species *Panax*, and are similar in their composition and properties. Ginseng is an adaptogen. It helps the body to return to its natural homeostasis after prolonged stress, illness, or upset. It promotes normalization of bodily functions, and regulates internal levels of hormones and enzymes. Ginseng also boosts concentration and mental performance.

Rosemary

Rosemary (*Rosmaryinus officinalis*) isn't just a good-tasting herb for use in cooking and baking; it also promotes vasodilation and peripheral blood flow. Rosemary contains carnosic acid, a powerful antioxidant, which counteracts the effect of cellular aging in the brain.[2] Antioxidants can protect the brain from stroke and degenerative neurological conditions like Alzheimer's disease. One of the folk names for rosemary is "the herb of remembrance," because it remedies poor memory, concentration difficulties, fatigue, and mental muddle.

Attention-deficit Hyperactivity Disorder

The occurrence of attention-deficit hyperactivity disorder (ADHD) is on the rise, affecting between three and five percent of all school-age children in North America. ADHD is more common in boys than in girls, and it appears to be hereditary with fathers passing it along to their children. In the majority of diagnoses, early prenatal health was cited as a contributing factor. Maternal drug, alcohol, and cigarette use, the exposure of the fetus to toxins like lead and polychlorinated biphenyls (PCBs), and nutritional deficiencies and imbalances may contribute to a propensity for ADHD behaviors in children.

ADHD is characterized by impulsive behavior, a lack of social control, hyperactivity, and a distinct lack of attention. Children with ADHD have a hard time organizing tasks, and

---

2. Sue Cartledge. "Rosemary Herb Helps Memory," at http://herbal-properties.suite101.com/article.cfm/heres_rosemary_for_remem brance#ixzz0QWmyF4Ql (accessed September 7, 2009.)

are easily distracted by outside stimuli. They forget routines, and resist tasks that seem complicated or require concentrated effort. Children with ADHD may also fidget or squirm, seem to be continually in motion, and appear unable to stay seated or keep their hands to themselves.

The behaviors are so persistent that they interfere with daily life, in particular the ability to function normally in the classroom, at home, and in usual social settings. While ADHD is primarily a childhood disease, symptoms sometimes persist into adult life. With treatment and intervention, the symptoms of the disorder can be reduced and many children with ADHD can lead productive lives.

Herbs that Help ADHD

A variety of herbs with both sedative and stimulating qualities are used to treat ADHD. While many are still being researched, the most commonly recommended are listed here.

Brahmi

Brahmi (*Bacopa monnieri*) is an Ayurvedic herb that has been long used in India and is becoming more well known in North America for the treatment of ADHD. It is considered to be a cognitive enhancer, stimulating improved learning and cognitive function. It also has antioxidant qualities, so it protects the brain from free-radical damage and the effects of aging and stress.

Gingko and Gotu Cola

Gingko (*Gingko biloba*) and gotu cola (*Centella asiatica*) are tonic herbs that promote increased blood flow and oxygen to the brain, normalizing neurological functions. They produce increased mental clarity, memory, and brain function, enabling a child with ADHD to process information and lessen feelings of being overwhelmed. Gotu cola also helps with emotional control and mood.

Siberian Ginseng

Siberian ginseng (*Eleutherococcus senticosus*) is an adaptogen that helps the body to return to normalized physiological function and to recover following illness or upset. With high antioxidant levels, Siberian ginseng helps to combat the effects of cellular aging and minimize stress. It stimulates brain activity, providing clarity and focus, and it normalizes the hypothalamus-pituitary-adrenal endocrine function.

For children who often feel overwhelmed by stimuli, Siberian ginseng can help slow them down, enable them to process data, and not be flooded with crazy-making stimuli.

Skullcap

Skullcap (*Scutellaria lateriflora*) and German chamomile (*Matricaria recutita*) both promote calm and relieve stress. They help a child with ADHD to slow down, diminishing feelings of overwhelm and confusion, promoting natural equilibrium, and normalizing brain function.

Last Words of Advice

Whatever you face, use your head. There are herbs that can help. But remember that no matter how much you read or know, you should always seek the advice of a qualified herbalist before taking herbs.

Ten Helpful Herbs for Fibromyalgia

⤜ by Katherine Weber-Turcotte ⤛

Fibromyalgia syndrome, often misunderstood or undiagnosed, affects millions of Americans each year. Women between the ages of twenty-five and fifty-five are ten times more likely to have fibromyalgia. While 90 percent of those affected by this baffling and painful syndrome are women, men and children are not immune to it.

Diagnosing fibromyalgia can be difficult. There are no specific lab or other diagnostic tests that are based on symptoms alone. The symptoms are widespread and range from fatigue (often chronic), insomnia and frequent night awakening, depression, headaches, decreased cognitive function or "fibro-fog," and joint and musculoskeletal pain throughout the entire body that often migrates from one area to another.

When broken down, *fibro* means "connective tissue" and *myalgia* means "muscle pain." Although somewhat related to arthritis, it does not damage the joints; it affects the soft tissues and muscles instead. Often considered by medical doctors to be a "waste basket" diagnoses, it is a disease that many suffer with daily. Although it is not life threatening, it can be exhausting and exasperating.

In 1990 the American College of Rheumatology wrote the first set of guidelines to help diagnose fibromyalgia. Diagnosis is most often confirmed by a rheumatologist. Certain criteria must be met to accurately diagnose fibromyalgia that include a collection of symptoms lasting over a period of time, and specific tender points on the body in the regions of the neck, spine, shoulders, elbows, and hips will confirm the diagnosis.

To date, no exact cause of fibromyalgia has been identified, but there are many possible triggers, including stress, injury or trauma, CFS (chronic fatigue syndrome), depression, undiagnosed Lyme disease, and a host of others, including viruses and autoimmune disorders such as rheumatoid arthritis and lupus. Heredity may also play a role. Fibromyalgia is not anything new; it is believed to have been around since the 1800s but was referred to as "muscular rheumatism." It later became known as "fibrositis," and in 1976 it became fibromyalgia.

Once the diagnosis has been confirmed, you will find ways to cope with your condition. This may include being under the care of a rheumatologist. Medication is not your only option or treatment, however. Proper rest and nutrition are the key factors in continuing to function with fibromyalgia. Patient education, exercise, self-management, and alternative therapies will also play a major role.

Alternative Treatments

Alternative medicine has much to offer the often desperate patient who tires of or finds little relief in conventional medicine and treatment. This can include such things as acupuncture, chiropractic, therapeutic massage, biofeedback, and herbal remedies.

Some of the following herbs are excellent choices to explore as you find a regime of care that is best suited to your individual needs. Before beginning any herbal treatment or supplement, though, consult with your primary physician.

Ashwagandha

Ashwagandha, also known as winter cherry (*Withania somnifera*), is native to drier, subtropical regions of India, Pakistan, Sri Lanka, and part of Africa. It can also be grown as an annual in temperate climates. Start indoors and set outside in full sun and well-drained soil after danger of frost has passed. Gather the roots in the fall.

An adaptogen herb with antistress qualities, ashwagandha also serves to enhance the immune system and provide antioxidant nutrients. A calming adaptogen, it works as an antispasmodic, nervine, antitumor, and anti-inflammatory, as well as having other medicinal properties.

Ashwagandha is an excellent choice if you suffer from fatigue, anxiety, fibro-fog, insomnia, muscle pain, or nervous exhaustion, or if you have auto-immune diseases such as chronic fatigue and rheumatoid arthritis. Taken in combination with kadzu root (*Pueraria lobata*), cyperus root (*Cyperus rotundus*), and black cohosh root (*Cimicifuga racemosa*), it can be used for the deep-muscle pain of fibromyalgia.

It can be taken as a tincture, decoction, or capsule, but check with a physician before using.

Chamomile

Chamomile has both an annual (*Matricaria recutita*) and a perennial (*Chamaemelum nobile)* variety. This herbaceous plant requires full sun to partial shade and prefers well-drained soil. Both the annual and perennial varieties can be grown in the home garden with little trouble, and the mature flowering tops are used in herbal medicine.

A nervine tonic, sedative, carminative, and antispasmodic (to name just a few of its medicinal properties), chamomile is often used to counteract the effects of stress. The essential oil of chamomile flowers (available through herbal mail order) acts as a potent anti-inflammatory. Adding chamomile to essential oil for massages will also help to soothe achy muscles.

The best and most effective use of chamomile is as an infusion. It can also be taken as a tisane/tea, tincture, or decoction. And a combination of chamomile, valerian, and passionflower may be used to improve sleep quality. Take as a medicinal honey to relieve headaches.

Note: if you are allergic to ragweed, be cautious about using chamomile.

Devil's Claw

Devil's claw (*Harpagophytum procumbens*) is native to southern Africa. Its name comes from its shape, which is a clawlike hand. The roots are used in herbal medicine and preparations.

Devil's claw can be taken as a tea/tincture or used as an external ointment/salve for pain. An anti-inflammatory, it is useful in the treatment of arthritis and rheumatic-type pain, neck and back pain, osteoarthritis, and also tendonitis.

A study done on Devil's claw (published in *The Journal of Rheumatology*) compared its effectiveness to the Cox-2 anti-inflammatory drug, Vioxx, which was removed from the market. It appears to work in the same manner with less side effects.

Note: use under the supervision of a physician.

Echinacea

Also known as purple coneflower (*Echinacea purpurea, E. angustifolia*, and *E. pallida*), echinacea is an easy-to-grow herbaceous perennial for the home garden. It likes full sun. The roots (when two and a half to three years old), leaves, and flowers are used in herbal medicine. Aerial parts may be harvested in the second year of growth. It is the most researched plant in the modern world, but in its wild habitat, it has become endangered due to overharvesting. Therefore, use only organically cultivated echinacea.

An immune system booster and anti-inflammatory, it may be taken as a tea, decoction, infusion, tincture (the entire plant), or in dried, powdered, and encapsulated form. Tincture with ginger is a powerful virus fighter, or make a syrup/elixir of both to help stave off colds. However, used continuously, it will lose effectiveness. It is best to use echinacea in cycles, such as five days on and two days off, until the problem has subsided.

Elderberry

Grow only the variety of elderberry (*Sambucus nigra*) with black/blue berries to use in herbal preparations. This easy-to-grow shrub has clusters of white flowers in summer and tiny black berries in the fall (raw fruit of *Sambucus nigra* may cause stomach upset). Both the flowers and berries are used medicinally, and the leaves may be used in making an elder leaf ointment to use for sprains.

A powerful diaphoretic, elderberry flower tea induces sweating and thus reduces fevers. It is a potent immune system booster and most useful in the flu-season months.

Eleuthero

Formerly called Siberian ginseng, eleuthero (*Eleutherococcus setaceous*) is not in the *Panax* ginseng family. Eleuthero grows throughout the regions of Siberia, northern China, Korea, and northern Japan. The root and stem bark are used in herbal medicine.

As an adaptogen, eleuthero helps to increase endurance and stamina while it strengthens the immune system. It also acts as a nervine to help those with insomnia and frequent nighttime awakening. Eleuthero may also be recommended for those with ADHD, chronic fatigue, immune deficiency, and adrenal fatigue.

Eleuthero can be combined effectively with other herbs for specific treatments. It may be taken as part of an herbal tonic, tincture, decoction, or fluid extract.

Note: if you are under a physician's care or on prescription medications, please consult with your physician before taking.

Licorice Root

A native plant to southeastern Europe and southwestern Asia, licorice root (*Glycyrrhiza glabra*, *G. uralensis*) grown in Spain and Italy is the most commercial variety used today. The Latin name for this plant is derived from the Greek words *glukos*, which means "sweet," and *riza*, which means "root."

Licorice root is used for a multitude of ailments. It is a remedy for respiratory problems, a soothing demulcent, a treatment for coughs, sore throat, and bronchial problems, as well as for gastrointestinal disorders such as ulcers.

It has the properties of being an adaptogen, antiviral, antihistamine, anti-inflammatory, antioxidant, and a host of other useful properties.

As an adaptogen herb, it is especially beneficial for those who suffer from adrenal exhaustion, depression, lethargy, and fatigue. It is also useful against wasting and debilitating diseases, and its property of being an immunomodulator helps to stimulate the immune system and also reduce excessive immune system response.

Best used when combined with other herbs in a multi herb formula, it can be taken in the form of a tea, tincture, decoction, or tablet, as well as a formula mixed with other beneficial herbs.

Note: caution should be used if you have high blood pressure and are on prescription medications. Check with a physician first.

Milky Oats

The immature seed of the common oat (*Avena sativa*) is filled with white "milk" for one week out of the growing cycle. It is in this stage that it is harvested and can be made into a fresh tincture, or glycerite.

Milky oats is an excellent tonic for the entire nervous system, helping to restore frayed nerves and a sense of calm and tranquility. Especially useful for those with chronic fatigue and panic disorders. Helpful for those with depression and insomnia.

Valerian

The medicinal value of valerian (*Valeriana officinalis*) has been known for centuries, thus making it one of the most popular herbal medicines in the world.

This is an easily grown herbaceous perennial that will grow in full sun, partial (preferred), or complete shade. Some may find the odor of valerian root rather pungent and unpleasant while the flowers are quite nicely scented. The roots may be harvested in the fall of the first year of growth, or the spring of the second.

Valerian has a strong sedative and pain relieving action. It is safe, effective and nonaddictive; however, there are those who react negatively to this if they are sensitive to the plant. While this sensitivity may be rare, if you feel greater agitation after taking valerian, discontinue using it.

It is useful for those suffering from stress, insomnia, pain from muscle spasms, tension, headaches, and other such issues. Best taken in the form of a decoction or a tincture.

Willow Bark

The bark of the willow tree (*Salix alba*) contains salicin, which converts to salicylic acid in the stomach. Does not cause gastrointestinal injury as does synthetically produced aspirin. Meadowsweet (*Filipendula ulmaria*), a similar herb, actually helps protect the stomach from ulcers.

The analgesic action of willow bark makes it useful for all types of pain. Can be used as a decoction/infusion. Fluid tinctures and extracts are also available from medical herbalists.

Herbs for Energy

⮞ by Sally Cragin ⮜

Tired, tired, so tired . . . Do I want (another) cup of coffee or a peanut butter sandwich? What I need is a pick-me-up. Should I stretch and take a brisk walk? Or maybe a protein bar—or something with red fruits, like goji berry?

So many of us pack more activity into a day than we can reasonably (or rationally) complete. But the body has been slowly evolving for just a hundred thousand years, and there are "lull" times when the body just wants to rest. For the past several years, I've written articles for the *Herbal Almanac* on kids' crafts and cosmetics, but this year, with the birth of my daughter, the issue that preoccupied me was how could I get more energy—now!

Was there food I should be eating (or not eating)? Were there herbs or other natural substances that would be helpful in getting through our days? Life with a tiny one put me on a different timetable—I had more in common with astronauts on the space shuttle, or scientists in Antarctica during winter. Time was no longer measurable in eight-hour increments—we were on that every three- to four-hour schedule. I have a scientist cousin who is capable of impressive feats of wakefulness (he's on a thirty-six-hour schedule naturally), but I could feel my body rebelling.

Solving an Energy Crisis

Fortunately, this state of affairs put me in a state of mind receptive to experimentation. What herbs, plants, vegetables, and supplements could help with my low energy level?

First Stop: Talk to a Nutritionist

June House, RN, is a holistic health nutritional counselor based in Massachusetts. Her first step with a new client is to do a detailed interview that includes questions about activities, food consumption, times of day when eating occurs, and other factors. "I find that some people need protein first thing in the morning," she said, "so I advise them to eat eggs or a green protein drink, something with spirulina or blue-green algae. But some people eat fruit and they feel fine."

Knowing your body type and what you need to feel good is essential if you are embarking on a program to enhance health and energy. "People are always looking for something new, so we go through these fads," says House. "We need things in our diets, but people are always reaching for pills when cultured vegetables are really easy to make." House recommends immediately excluding processed foods, including sugar and white flour, from the diet. "I ask people: How do you feel after you eat something sugary?" Someone will say, 'I feel great, but an hour later I feel hungry and my energy feels low.'"

So what do you want to put *in* you to get more energy *out* of you? What follows is a somewhat subjective, personally tested array of products, herbs, and compounds that I've found helpful. I recommend checking with a nutritionist or your doctor if you have pronounced symptoms.

Energy Options

Bee Products

There are more of these than you might think: honey (produced by bees as food), bee pollen (gathered by bees for a food source), and royal jelly (produced for creating a new queen in the hive). Since well before Old Testament times, bee products have been touted as everything from balm, to antiseptic, to energy source, and honey is definitely easier on the nerves than processed sugar.

British author Roald Dahl wrote an amazing story called "Royal Jelly" in which well-meaning parents wanted to feed their human baby the best and most nutritious food: royal jelly. And the jelly was a huge success until the parents started noticing yellow and black stripes on their beloved babe.

But in the real world, honey, royal jelly, and bee pollen are time-tested supplements, to judge from myriad manufacturers touting their benefits. Despite the lack of official findings, royal jelly (which is fed to the bee larvae by the sister-mothers in the hive) for humans is said to have immune-system boosting properties. Bee pollen is a natural product I've recently started adding to smoothies (see below). I can't say that it's giving me more energy, but I'm willing to keep using it as this has an interesting taste. Plus, bee pollen is a "whole food" that is rich in protein.

Fiber

So simple! Vegetables, fruits, whole grains, you know the drill. Fiber keeps your body working, staves off constipation, and is good for the colon. So a high-fiber diet will help you keep your energy up. If you're under fifty, the recommended amount is 25 grams a day for women and 38 grams a day for men (sources: mayoclinic.com, and yes those are the highest recommendations I found; the British recommendations are just half that). Getting up to 25 grams is a challenge, but since many fruits and vegetables (per cup) are between 4 and 6 grams, getting five servings of fruits and vegetables a day will be good for your blood sugar and will help to keep your energy up as well as being healthy for you! Raspberries (the best summer fruit ever!) are high-fiber: 8 grams per cup. If you peel a couple of carrots and cut them in sticks, each four to five sticks is nearly 2 grams of fiber.

Chocolate!

Okay, now we're talking about energy! Yes, it is a nut, so it is a food! Seriously, though, if you want the most efficient kind of chocolate as an energy boost, look for 70 percent cocoa and above, which means more expensive, but truly yummy artisanal chocolate bars. In the eighteenth century, a chocolate drink was part of a light breakfast (although soon supplanted by coffee and tea).

Coffee

Some years back, I started ordering tea at restaurants instead of coffee, primarily because it's easy to screw up a good cup of coffee, and it's hard to make tea come out wrong. But our fascination with coffee goes back centuries and, by 1700, when the Atlantic trade routes were well-established, there were more than two thousand coffee houses in London. And from coffee houses came lengthy and voluminous political and literary discussions from the coffee drinkers. Coffee will definitely provide energy, and learning how much coffee you can drink, and at what point in the day (with food? or without?) is a good experiment. In the last ten years, thanks to the coffee company with "Star" in the name, the idea of "good coffee" has been revolutionized.

Goji Berry

"This came in ten years ago," says Rafael Avila, the manager of research and development for Nature's Plus, a manufacturer of a wide range of products. Nature's Plus added goji berry as an ingredient to their energy supplements after a variety of studies. Goji berry is also known as Chinese wolfberry, and it grows in the Himalayas. It is used in traditional Chinese medicine and is said to help the immune system, eyesight, and circulation, among other benefits.

Green Tea

Personally, I like the taste of powdered green tea. Ideally, someone else is calmly mixing the powder into a hand-thrown porcelain bowl and then frothing up the brew with a bamboo whisk while I sit on a gracefully upholstered cushion, watching. Green tea is all about the process, not just the consumption. I try to make green tea in a small teapot so I can drink it from a raku-fired ceramic cup. It is so much more gracious than supping from a mass-marketed glazed coffee cup with the name of the bank you had three accounts ago.

Kava-kava

The kava-kava root comes from the Pacific islands and is an integral part of folk ritual and socializing in that part of the world. Many commercial products advertise its benefits as an anti-stress medication, but there are also concerns about potential side effects to the liver if too much is used. The root is powdered and consumed in a drink, although a hot drink can weaken the effects. I've tried kava-kava, but I think this is another of those situations where—if I were visiting the island of Vanatu, and sitting on the beach drinking out of a coconut, I'd get the effects more.

Lycopene

Lycopene is found in tomatoes, spaghetti sauce, bright red veggies, papaya, and watermelon. It is an antioxidant that is said to have cancer-prevention properties although this claim has not been proven. Lycopene is also one of the ingredients in a product I've liked as an afternoon pick-me-up, "Nature's Plus Source of Life Red," which is a vitamin, mineral, and protein energy shake that is made by the aforementioned Nature's Plus. "Shortly after we introduced the Source of Life products, we started to get feedback that people were reporting a burst of energy," explains Avila. So the company expanded into other varieties of supplements and products. "We've been relying on the effects of spirulina —that has been great for twenty-five years, but we've seen other whole foods have expanded," he says. "We've been exploring the energizing affects."

Maca

This Peruvian herb is grown at elevations of about 14,000 feet and was rediscovered by the developed world in recent years. The root is ground and consumed in a tincture, and the plant is also edible. I'm intrigued by maca as it is said to have energy-producing, depression-relieving, aphrodisiacal properties. Some people whose opinion I respect when it comes to herbal knowledge swear by it, but I haven't had consistent results personally. It's a quirky little plant that grows in very rough terrain and commercial preparations include tablets and powders. It's related to the radish family (also turnip) and this is one I'm curious about exploring further once my daughter and I are past the nursing stage.

Peppermint

Smell the crushed leaves, put some peppermint oil on pulse spots, or have a cup of peppermint tea. This tangy and versatile plant is one of my favorites, and lots of fun to experiment with.

Protein

Increasing your protein (and fiber; see above) can help your energy during the day. A handful of nuts gives me a longer-lasting feeling of satisfaction than a handful of raisins or dried cranberries (though nuts and dried fruit together are a better team than separated).

Spirulina or Blue-green Algae

The health sources and practitioners I spoke to swore by this, and I'm willing to keep an open mind. As I write this article,

I'm adding blue-green algae to various smoothies I concoct.
I like the earthy/plantlike taste, but then, I'm someone who
finds Chanel No. 5 overwhelmingly whiffy and don't mind a
faint aroma of skunk in the woods.

Tobacco

Yes, you're shocked! And no, we're not recommending this.
But it's an interesting choice for many cultures. Think about
how Europeans first learned about tobacco, from the New
World and from the Near East. Putting a little bit of 'bakky
into a pipe (water pipe or otherwise) would get you a jolt of
energy, as well as soporific effects. Smoking—passing the peace
pipe, for example—is a sacred act among many North American
tribes. Of course, its strong addictive, cancer-causing properties
outweigh the benefits. I know a career service person who only
smokes when he's "in country," for the relaxing effects. Oscar
Wilde summed up the weed's essential nature when he com-
mented, "Smoking is the perfect pleasure; it always leaves you
unsatisfied." (No, we are not recommending this!)

Other Methods for Increasing Energy

Nutritionist June House advises clients to eat "according to
the seasons." To keep it simple: in the summer when it's hot,
eat cool, light food. In the winter, when it's not, eat hot, more
substantial meals. "Here in New England, in the fall, we get
all our squashes, for example," says House. "The colder it
gets, the warmer foods we want. Those root vegetables, Hub-
bard squashes, and carrots are good for our bodies then. In the
spring and summer, we want to eat lighter."

House notes that in a less temperate climate, eating fruit
for a longer period of the year may be a healthier option. "My

teacher in India told me a story about seeing a poor man. He offered him fruit, and even though it was winter (so in India, it was 70 degrees) the man said, 'I don't eat fruit at this time, because my body will get cold.' But we've lost that connection to how food affects our temperature and how our bodies feel."

Eat Dark Green Leafy Vegetables

According to House, the chlorophyll in those foods and the blue-green algae realm is a close match for our blood chemistry, "so it's nourishing to the body." But not everything that's green will give you the health and energizing benefits of dark green vegetables. "People don't eat enough of the good green things," she says. "People think eating iceberg lettuce is good because it's a green food, but it's mostly water." House recommends swiss chard, kale, and collard greens. In my experience, if the taste of these plants needs some help, toasted sesame seeds or toasted almond seeds go a long way to make these veggies more palatable.

Easy Smoothies for an Energy Boost

Ever since uncovering a gorgeous old glass Waring blender that was a wedding present from my parents, I've been on a smoothies kick. I also have a juicer, which I love, but there are more parts to clean. A blender is fine for simple juicing procedures.

Late one summer I had a cold that just wouldn't quit. I immediately cut all dairy from my diet. No cheese, no milk with cereal, no bowl of ice cream during *Law and Order*. After a few days, I noticed my sinuses were behaving better. I started adapting some of the smoothies to be fast and simple, and to incorporate what I already had in the larder. I love reading recipes in high-end magazines, which require trips to specialty grocery stores, candy thermometers, and multiple days to prepare. But with a wee baby strapped to my hip, it's a lot easier to make something with ingredients already on hand. ("Spoon" usually refers to a flatware tablespoon. Where *did* the measuring spoons go to? Oh, right, toys for the baby . . .)

No Frills Late-morning Smoothie

¼ to ½ cup wheat germ, or crunchy cereal

1 chopped ripe banana

1 teaspoon of bee pollen (optional)

2 cups rice, almond, or cow's milk (or water, which can thickened with a spoonful of yogurt)

1 big spoonful of peanut butter

Edible vegetables (of your choice)

Directions:

1. Soak wheat germ (or cereal) in the liquid for 10 minutes before blending.

2. Peel a cucumber, quarter it, and remove seeds. Put in blender.

3. Dice a tomato.

4. Add enough tomato or vegetable juice (or water, but as noted, that's a little meager), orange or fruit juice to make two cups.

5. Blend on high; add pepper if needed.

6. Options: peeled diced celery, peeled chopped carrots, or green beans. There will make a veggie slush at the bottom of the glass, but the vegetables will perk up the flavor and give you a jolt of antioxidants.

Herbal Aphrodisiacs

≈ by Katherine Weber-Turcotte ≈

The dictionary defines an aphrodisiac as a food, drug, potion, or other agent that arouses sexual desire. Derived from the Greek word *aphrodisiakos*, it pertains to Aphrodite, the Greek goddess of love and beauty.

The use of aphrodisiacs goes back at least sixty thousand years. Hippocrates, the "father of medicine," recommended indulging in lentils well into old age as it was thought that they kept an older man alert and at attention. Fassolatha, a bean soup, is the national dish of Greece and believed to be a great aphrodisiac. Other early aphrodisiacs included marinated edible bulbs mixed with honey and sesame seeds, and also garlic and onions, which were consumed on a regular basis. Spain is famous for bull's testicles and people in the Far East still consider a rhino's horn a great booster for a man's sex drive. Although rhino horns are illegal, the belief and practice still continues today.

The Doctrine of Signatures said that the shape of a root, vegetable, or fruit would be an aphrodisiac if it resembled the human genitalia (phallic-shaped for men and soft and moist for women). This could be anything from bananas, figs, cucumbers, even avocados that hung in pairs off a tree. Partaking in eating the genitalia of virile animals that copulated prolifically, such as bulls and rams, was also thought to ensure a man an extra boost in the bedroom. It doesn't take a great imagination to associate certain foods with body parts.

Many legendary aphrodisiacs were from the sea. The Greek goddess Aphrodite was herself a gift of the sea. Oysters, eels, and clams were, therefore, regarded as potent aphrodisiacs. This is true in many cases. Oysters (a prime source of zinc) and shrimp (a source of iodine) contain the minerals and nutrients that promote a strong libido. Legend has it that the famed lover, Casanova, ate fifty raw oysters each day for breakfast.

Eventually, some plants became recognized for their ability to produce increased energy and sexual vigor among users. Once again, this can be tied in to the fact that many of these plants contained essential vitamins and minerals that helped the body to function properly.

What Causes a Lagging Libido?

Sexual dysfunction can be caused by a myriad of things ranging from physical illness, relationship changes, menstrual as well as midlife hormonal changes, fatigue, stress, anxiety, medications, or alcohol and drug abuse.

It is also important that you are not sabotaging your sex life with bad habits. Alcohol, tobacco, illicit drugs, and some prescription medications (such as antidepressants) and over-the-counter drugs (such as antihistamines) can cause sexual impairment. An unhealthy, high-fat, high-cholesterol diet can also wreak havoc with your sex life.

Before you consider using any aphrodisiac, it is essential that you check with your health-care provider. Before you purchase herbal products, make sure you are buying from a reliable source. And talk to others who are knowledgeable about herbs—your pharmacist, a naturopath, alternative health-care provider, even your own physician.

Remember that herbal products are not FDA approved (although some claim they are manufactured in an FDA approved plant). Do your homework and research a product thoroughly so you can ask questions. Be wary of products advertised on late-night television. Look for products that offer a guarantee, and read the fine print so you can be an informed buyer.

Form and Action of Aphrodisiacs

Aphrodisiacs can be consumed in a variety of ways: teas, infusions, decoctions, syrups, meads, and tinctures, and combined with other herbs/ingredients as herbal tonics. They can be eaten as a food or spice, or taken in pill or capsule form. They can be burned as an incense or smudge, and some can be smoked. They can be applied directly to the body in scented oils, ointments, and salves. Candles are another way to benefit from the sensuality of scent.

An aphrodisiac works by increasing blood flow to sexual organs to prolong or enhance sexual arousal. They can also mimic male and female sex hormones and increase the amount of testosterone (the hormone responsible for sexual desire) in the blood. They also work by improving the nerve endings and nerve conduction in the parts of the brain responsible for controlling pleasure, thus heightening the sensation of touch.

Herbal Aphrodisiacs

Damiana

Damiana (*Turnera diffusa*) is a small shrublike plant that is native to Mexico and the dry, sandy, and rocky places of the southwestern United States. Used as an old Mexican folk remedy to treat various urinary as well as sexual problems, it is also useful for treating fatigue, bronchial irritation, and urinary problems.

Although, primarily thought of as an aphrodisiac for women, dimiana is believed to increase the sensitivity of both the clitoris and penis (it may cause premature ejaculation in some men). It is used today to treat women with a low sex drive as well as for urinary and vaginal infections and for some menstrual problems. Damiana contains alkaloids similar to caffeine that stimulate blood flow to the genitals and thus increase sensitivity. Widely available, it can be taken as a tea, pill, or extract/tincture; it is often incorporated into herbal formulas.

Although there are really no known side effects, it is possible that damiana may interfere with iron absorption in the body. While taking this herb, increase your intake of foods that are high in iron such as leafy, dark-green vegetables, eggs, nuts, red meats, and fruits.

Epimedium

Also known as horny goat weed (*Epimedium grandiflorum*, *E. koreanum*, *E. pinnatum*, *E. rubrum*), epimedium is the most powerful vegetarian herbal sexual tonic in Chinese herbal medicine. Epimedium, a leafy perennial, grows freely in countryside and high mountainous regions in China, where it is also known as yin-yang huo. Because only the leaves are harvested, it is not in danger of becoming overharvested.

Botanist James Duke is most responsible for introducing this herb in one of the bestselling herbal supplements of all time. It is often combined with other herbs in a formula for sexual enhancement. With a name like horny goat weed, it leaves little to the imagination!

It is used to restore sexual vigor, treat impotence as well as premature ejaculation, increase production of sperm, and strengthen connective tissue. The androgen-like effects stimulate sexual activity as well as increase sperm count and heighten sexual arousal.

It is also useful for women who are experiencing a lagging libido, as it contains testosterone-like substances that may increase the sex drive. It will not interfere with hormonal balance. It is also a powerful immunity booster and regulator and best when taken in a Chinese herbal formula.

Ginger

Ginger (*Zingiber officinale*) is derived from the root of the plant and is highly stimulating; it is available in any supermarket for fresh use. This root has been widely used in traditional Chinese medicine, Ayurvedic medicine, and Native American medicine.

Ginger is commonly used in cooking and baking, but it has also become increasingly recognized for its medicinal use. Ginger benefits the cardiovascular, digestive, and immune systems. It is interesting to note that the Koran says that ginger will promote digestion and "strengthen sexual activity."

No formal studies exist on the use of ginger as a sexual stimulant; however, it does cause a warming sensation that can be felt throughout the body. It acts as an adaptogen to help restore balance to the body. Its use as a cardiovascular tonic may support the belief that ginger helps the flow of blood to the sexual organs to increase sexual satisfaction. Ginger is also antibacterial, antiviral, anti-inflammatory, antifungal, analgesic, antitussive, antispasmodic, carminative, and antiarthritic.

Ginger may be used freshly grated and used for tea. It is simply delicious when grated or mashed and mixed with honey (a popular home remedy for a cough). It is also available candied as well as dried, pickled, in tablet or capsule form, or as an extract/tincture.

Note: ginger should not be used by anyone taking an anticoagulant or aspirin as it thins the blood.

Gingko

The leaves and nuts of gingko (*Gingko biloba*) have been used for thousands of years by the Chinese to increase sexual vigor, promote longevity, and treat a myriad of ailments from allergies and asthma to cancer. A deciduous ornamental tree, gingko is often referred to as the "smart herb," and it is recognized as an antioxidant that protects cell membranes in the brain and other body organs from "free radical" damage that can cause cancer.

Without the danger of increasing blood pressure, gingko has the ability to improve blood flow to all vital organs and tissues of the body. Its ability to increase circulation has helped gingko become recognized as an anti-aging herb that helps those with poor concentration, impaired memory, and depression. It is thought by some that gingko may also slow the progression of Alzheimer's disease. By increasing the blood flow to the genitals, it is an excellent choice as a sexual booster and also as a treatment for impotence.

Gingko is widely available and comes in pill and extract forms as well as being an ingredient in other herbal products. It is important to note that it may take several months to notice the positive effect of gingko. It is suggested that gingko be taken in a standardized form.

Note: if you are on a blood thinner or take aspirin daily, avoid using this herb.

Ginseng

Ginseng (*Panax ginseng, Panax quinquefolius*) is native to northeast China, Korea, and Russia. This slow-growing perennial takes approximately six years to produce a mature root. *Panax* is derived from the Greek words *panacea* and *akos*, which translate as "cure." Esteemed sixteenth-century physician Li Shihchen touted ginseng root as an aphrodisiac and love potion.

Regular use of ginseng nourishes and energizes the reproductive organs, thus bringing a return to vital energy in both men and women. Continued use will raise sperm motility and ensure a hard erection. The tonic effect of ginseng acts on the pituitary, thus activating the adrenal glands, which gives it an adaptogen effect. Chinese ginseng stimulates nitric oxide (reported in 1997 by a professor at Yale University's School of Medicine), a neurotransmitter that mediates a variety of bodily actions, one of which is dilation of the blood vessels. An enzyme is activated by the nitric oxide that relaxes smooth muscle and allows blood to flow. When this action occurs in the penis, an erection can result. The prescription drug Viagra works by the same concept; however, Viagra comes with side effects.

For menopausal women, ginseng can be a godsend. Its regular use will help to relieve hot flashes, night sweats, menopausal headaches, insomnia, and also mood swings.

Ginseng is a friend to those with adrenal exhaustion. Its regular use will help to combat fatigue and help you to regain your stamina and vitality. Other benefits include improved memory, and a greater ability to concentrate. Ginseng can also help to protect the heart and cardiovascular system; it may stave off diabetes and help protect against cancer.

Ginseng is available in a variety of forms as well as in herbal tonics. Since ginseng is overharvested, it is important to purchase your ginseng from a reliable source, because some unscrupulous manufacturers adulterate their products.

Note: check with your health-care practitioner before taking ginseng. Do not take ginseng if you are on anticoagulants or aspirin.

Oatstraw

Who has not heard the phrase, "Sowing your wild oats"? There is much truth behind the benefits that can be had by partaking of oatstraw (*Avena sativa*). This annual grass is used when it is still green, before the grain ripens, for the most beneficial results.

Taking oatstraw as an infusion or tincture is most beneficial. A lovely infusion can be made by mixing oatstraw with some red clover and nettles. Menopausal women who are experiencing nervous exhaustion and insomnia will find oatstraw to be a very useful herb. Wild oats contain alkaloids that are believed to be responsible for their relaxing action.

Oatstraw is loaded with calcium and magnesium and it will help to strengthen your bones and protect against osteoporosis. It is excellent for improving the complexion and growing strong nails and hair. Consistent use of oatstraw is beneficial to your heart and will help you to maintain lower blood pressure and cholesterol. Rich in phytosterol, your endocrine system and hormones will be well balanced with oatstraw use. And did I mention that oatstraw tastes wonderful and is a great booster to your libido?

Saw Palmetto

A small, shrubby palm tree with sword-shaped leaves and sweet, nutritive tonic berries, Saw palmetto (*Serenoa serrulata*) is native to the southwest region of the United States. Known for centuries as a medicinal tonic, it was highly regarded by the Native Americans. Today, it is widely used in alternative medicine.

Saw palmetto acts as an antiseptic to the urinary tract, making it an excellent choice for acute or chronic urinary problems. It also tones and strengthens the bladder and is a great herb for those experiencing prostate problems. It is known to reduce swelling in cases of benign prostatic hypertrophy (BPH).

It nourishes the reproductive system as well as the endocrine glands and is strongly indicated for its reputation as an aphrodisiac. The phytosterol-rich berries help to bring vitality to the sex organs and its ability to act as a tissue builder and moisturizer to rebuild and revamp dry or atrophied tissue.

Widely available and taken as pills, extracts and tea, saw palmetto is often combined synergistically with other herbs.

Heal Your Animals
with Herbs

☙ by Suzanne Ress ☙

Only relatively recently has medical science "discovered" that many of the ancient herbal cures, passed on from shaman to herbal healer to housewife throughout millennia, actually do contain valuable chemical properties. Some of these ancient cures have been put through laboratory tests, which proved them can prevent, heal, and cure a wide variety of health problems.

Since the first century AD, the bark of the white willow tree (*Salix alba*) boiled in water to form a decoction has been effectively used as a fever reducer, a painkiller, and as an aid to ease rheumatoid arthritis. Not until the late 1890s was it discovered that acetylsalicylic acid (otherwise known as aspirin), which is derived from the bark of the willow tree, is probably the world's most effective pain reliever and fever reducer.

Other scientifically recognized herbal remedies available in modern pharmaceuticals include:

- Deadly nightshade (*Atropa belladonna*), which is used for Parkinson's disease and epilepsy, and in the eye drops ophthalmologists use to dilate their patient's pupils.

- Ephedra is prescribed for asthma and emphysema.

- Opium poppy (*Papaver somniferum*) is used to produce morphine, codeine, thebaine, and other strong prescription narcotic pain killers.

- Oil of thyme (*Thymus vulgaris*) is a disinfectant ingredient in many cleaning products, toothpastes, and mouthwashes.

These are just a few of the herbs and plants with valuable and potent active chemical ingredients that can heal or cure, and, if abused or used carelessly, even kill a human being.

People who have taken an interest in herbal cures as an alternative to synthetic laboratory-made medicines for themselves might also consider using herbal medicines for their pets.

Herbal Cures for Your Animals

Horses are particularly interesting candidates for herbal cures since their natural diet consists of grass and herbs. If left to fend for themselves in a large enough open area with a wide variety of edible plants to choose from, horses know by instinct which herbs to eat to maintain good health, or to cure or help heal general health problems and injuries.

Many, if not most, modern domestic horses are kept in artificial environments and fed a standard ration of hay and sweet feed. As a result, stable-kept horses are likely to develop health problems such as allergies, asthma, colic, and habitual behaviors, considered vices, due to their greatly reduced chewing activity.

There is a lot that can be done by using fresh and dried herbal supplements and extractions to improve the health of these noble grazing animals. The difficulty lies in knowing what and how much to give an individual horse for its particular problem, which has, hopefully, been correctly diagnosed.

Although many people consider dogs to be carnivores, in nature, wild canines do eat berries and certain fruits. And what dog owner has not witnessed his pet gnawing off tufts of coarse grass, usually couchgrass (*Elymus repens*), only to promptly vomit it up again? Wild canines such as wolves, coyotes, and foxes all exhibit this same behavior, which is believed to be a form of self-medication to relieve stomach upset or mild urinary tract infections. Couchgrass contains a natural antibiotic substance known to help cure urethritis, cystitis, and other urinary tract problems in canines.

Though you can't very easily convince a dog to eat a bowl full of raw herbs, small amounts of decoctions, infusions, and finely chopped fresh or dried (and crumbled or powdered) herbs can be mixed into a dog's regular food. Most dogs will be perfectly willing to let you apply poultices, compresses, oils, or ointments to various parts of their bodies.

Besides their natural attraction to catnip (*Nepeta cataria*) for its narcotic effects, cats seems to enjoy inhaling the aroma of other herbs such as valerian (*Valeriana officinalis*), which is a sedative, and thyme, a natural antiseptic and insect repellent. Since cats are sometimes picky eaters, it could be pretty tricky to get some of them to ingest even a small amount of herbs or herbal infusion, even when it's concealed in their favorite food. In such cases, appropriate amounts of dried powdered herbs can be put into small gelatin capsules, and the capsule tossed down the cat's throat whole. All you can do is try and if you have no success in the matter, try a cold or hot compress instead.

Diagnose First

So much depends upon making the correct diagnosis to begin with, which is not always easy, since animals don't talk to us. Remember that the herbal cures written about in this article should be thought of as general guidelines only! Readers are strongly advised to consult with a qualified veterinarian, preferably one familiar with and sympathetic to alternative medicines, before trying out any of the following treatments on an animal.

Once a diagnosis is made, you must make sure to administer the proper treatment/dosage according to the individual animal's age, size, and condition. Keep in mind that a small dog or cat is often no heavier than a newborn human infant, so dosages must be very small, and potency minimal.

Dogs, even small ones, are able to tolerate a much wider variety of herbs and herbal treatments than cats, but always be mindful of their body weight. Even large dogs often weigh less than a twelve-year-old child, so be careful of the strength of the cures you give them.

Herbal Preparations

There are various ways of preparing herbs to be used for healing purposes. Two of the most commonly used are infusions and decoctions.

Infusions

An infusion is like a strong herbal tea; the herbs, dried or fresh, must be steeped for 15 to 30 minutes in water that has been heated to boiling. If using fresh herbs, you'll need the following ingredients:

> 2 to 3 tablespoons of herbs
>
> 2½ cups water

If using dried herbs, you'll need:

> 1 tablespoon herbs
>
> 2½ cups water

Directions:

1. Never boil the herbs in the water. Place them, whether dried or fresh, in a ceramic teapot and pour the boiling water over them.
2. Cover the pot tightly and let the herbs steep. Strain before using.

Decoctions

A decoction, on the other hand, calls for gently boiling cleaned, crushed, or chopped herbs, fruits, berries, barks, coarse stems, or roots in pure water for about 30 minutes. For decoctions, use:

> 1 ounce of ingredients
>
> 4½ cups water in a nonreactive pan with a lid

Half of the water will have evaporated by the time 30 minutes has elapsed. Let cool completely before straining and using.

Ski-care Oils

Massage and general skin and hair/fur oils can be made by putting 2 ounces of dried and crushed herb, or 4 ounces of chopped fresh herb, into a glass jar with 1¼ cups olive, almond, or jojoba oil. Leave the jar in the sun for a week to allow the herbs to macerate and release their essential oils. Shake the jar occasionally. Then, strain and use.

Ointments

An ointment can be made by whipping 1 or 2 ounces of pure beeswax, melted, into the same amount of herbal oil. Let the mixture cool before using.

Poultice

To make a poultice, mix dried and crushed or fresh chopped herbs with enough hot water to form a paste. Apply this directly to the affected body part and cover with clean gauze or cotton wraps. Leave in place until the poultice is cold.

Compress

A compress can be either hot or cold, depending on its use. Soak a clean cotton dish towel in hot herbal tea, or in a cold herbal infusion, and place it on the affected body part for 20 to 30 minutes. This can be repeated as often as necessary.

In treating cats, please be aware that herbal essential oils are too strong for them and should never be used in any way, shape, or form. Use only teas, infusions or, in limited cases, fresh or dried herbs.

Treatments

Arthritis, Muscle Pain, and Headaches

For older animals with rheumatic arthritis, a tincture of devil's claw can be given orally to great effect. Devil's claw, which actually does resemble what it's named for, is the root of the flowering herbal plant *Harpagophytum procumbens*. It has been used for centuries in southern Africa and Madagascar to treat joint pains, and medical science has recently confirmed its effectiveness.

Mild decoctions of white willow bark, mother of acetyl-salicylic acid (aspirin), can be given to dogs and horses to ease muscle or joint pain, headaches, and to lower a fever. Dogs, however, like humans, may suffer mild stomach pain from ingesting the decoction. Cats should never be given any form of white willow bark as their bodies cannot metabolize salicylate, and this can result in hearing impairment.

Bathing

Bathing a nervous dog in warm water to which you've added two cups of valerian root and chamomile flower (*Chamaemelum nobile*) infusion should calm him enough so that he'll stay still.

Bad Breath

For bad breath there are several options. Licorice-scented fennel (*Foeniculum vulgare*) seed can be added to a dog's food. Besides freshening the breath, fennel seed aids digestion. Fresh raw parsley (*Petroselinum crispum*) is safe to feed to dogs, but you must make sure they chew it, because if they swallow it whole, it will not affect their breath. Some dogs like chewing on celery sticks and this is a fantastic breath freshener, too. Although celery is not an herb, it is closely related to lovage (*Levisticum officinale*), which works just as well, but perhaps dogs prefer something "chewier." Remove the tough strings from the celery stalk before giving it to your dog, however, because he can't digest the fibrous strings and they could block his intestine. An added benefit of celery, as well as lovage, is that they are very good for stiff joints.

Eye Problems

A warm compress of rosemary and meadowsweet (*Filipendula ulmaria*) can be held against a dog's eyes if he has an eye infection. Try to do this when he's feeling sleepy and relaxed. It should be held in place 10 to 20 minutes at a time.

Not actually an herb, though used as one in some Mexican dishes, pumpkin seed (*Cucurbita pepo*) has proven to be a very effective wormer for dogs. Grind up the raw seeds and add a heaping tablespoon to his food for several days.

Flea and Tick Control

To discourage fleas from taking up residence in your cat's sleeping area, keep the area and bedding very clean, and strew fresh rosemary (*Rosmarinus officinalis*) sprigs underneath her mat or cushion. Make sure she doesn't eat them, because rosemary can be toxic to cats!

A gentle infusion of calendula (*Calendula officinalis*) and mullein (*Verbascum thapsus*) can be put into a small glass spray bottle and used carefully around the cat's ears to rid them of mites and excess wax.

Limited amounts of garlic also help to repel ticks and fleas. Additionally, you might try tying a sprig of rosemary, eucalyptus, or geranium leaf to your dog's collar. Just remember to put a fresh one on each day. You can also make an oil, using 2 or 3 drops of lavender and cedarwood essential oils in 2 tablespoons of olive oil. Massage the oil into the fur on his back, between his shoulders, once every few days.

Hairball Remedy

As an effective cure for hairballs, *Plantago Psyllium nigrum* husk, which comes from the coarse desert Indianwheat (*Plantago ovata*), is a natural laxative, and can be given, either mixed into the cat's food with a small amount of wheat germ oil or in capsule form.

Insect Bites

To relieve the pain of bee stings and insect bites, poison ivy, and minor cuts, make an ointment with calendula flower petals. Fresh aloe gel is also useful for these same problems.

Motion Sickness

If your dog suffers motion sickness while traveling, try giving him a small piece of candied ginger (*Zingiber officinale*) to settle his stomach and combat nausea.

Stomach Aches

The tops of catnip can be used fresh or dried to make an infusion that calms stomach upsets. It will also work as a mild sedative.

Urinary Tract Infections

As a cure for cats' urinary tract infections, try giving a tea made of couch grass root. Another very effective and safe urinary tract cure is an infusion made of bearberries (*uva Arctostaphylos ursi*), and the seeds of stavesacre (*Delphinium staphisagria*). If possible, the cat must drink this infusion in place of water or other liquids until the infection clears up.

Worms

A preventative treatment against worms is garlic (*Allium sativum*), either finely chopped raw or dehydrated flakes or powder. Do not continue giving a dog garlic for longer than a few days at a time, as it can lead to anemia.

Treatments for Horses

Horses can tolerate and benefit from most of the same herbs that humans can, plus some others that we cannot. There are some exceptions to this, though. Horses should never be given St. John's wort (*Hypericum perforatum*), an herb commonly used as a natural antibacterial, astringent, and even antidepressant in humans. If a horse ingests St. John's wort, he will suffer photosensitivity, making it impossible for him to tolerate natural sunlight.

Other herbs poisonous to horses are mare's tail grass (*Equisetum arvense*), which contains the enzyme thiaminase. This enzyme destroys thiamine (vitamin B1) in the horse's body, leading to tremors, loss of condition, and death.

Anxiety and Nervousness

Lemon balm (*Melissa officinalis*) is a mild sedative useful for treating nervous or anxious horses, and it has antifungal and antibacterial properties as well.

Colic

Dried chamomile flowers can be mixed into the feed as a sedative, and a half-bucket full of cooled chamomile tea can be given to a horse suffering mild colic to ease his discomfort.

Coughs

A warm poultice made of eucalyptus, thyme, and spearmint (*Mentha spicata*), applied to the horse's chest and neck, can help clear up a cough due to a cold.

Healthy Hooves

To keep a horse's hooves healthy, make up an oil using olive oil as the carrier, and include linseed oil and essential oils of wintergreen, comfrey, and lavender. With a soft cloth or a brush, cover the horse's hooves, including the soles and frogs, with a thin coating of this oil once a week.

Supplements to Aid Recovery

Fenugreek (*Trigonella foenum-graecum*) is a beanlike, grassy plant that is rich in iron, minerals, and vitamins; it is an excellent supplement food for thin or recovering horses.

The young spring leaf tops of stinging nettle are optimal for any animal's (including cats, dogs, horses, and humans) immune system. Stinging nettle (*Urtica dioica*) is packed with essential minerals, including calcium, phosphorus, iron, magnesium, potassium, and vitamin C. If only the small new leaves are collected (wearing gloves, just in case!) in the spring before the plant flowers, they should not sting. The fresh leaves can be made into a tea or an infusion, or dried for later use. Dried leaves can also be crumbled and mixed into food.

Whatever herbs you may use to heal an animal, please remember that before administering any treatment, no matter how innocuous it may seem, it is important to first get a diagnosis and professional opinion from a qualified veterinarian. Doing so could even mean the life of your pet.

Live a Natural Life with Herbal Pesticides

≫ by Misty Kuceris ≪

Sitting outside on my deck during the warm season is like being in a wooded parkland. It is on the second-floor level, and overlooks my backyard that is filled with hundred-year-old oak, ash, and beech trees and is bordered by a brook. When my friends and I sit and relax on the deck, we feel like we're in a special tree house that has a canopy of leaves to protect us from the summer's heat. We listen to the birds that come by for food. We watch the bats at dusk as they swoop past for their evening insect meals. We feel the breezes brush by our faces like waves of affection. Yet, what we don't feel while surrounded by all that nature

is the bites from mosquitoes that we know are out there. It's as if they don't exist. My deck, which is my oasis of relaxation and my warm season living room, is also my herb garden. Being surrounded by pots of basil, lemon verbena, lovage, oregano, thyme, and whatever else I'm growing that year provides a protection that repels unwanted insects yet attracts swallowtail butterflies and other beneficial insects that pollinate the rest of my land.

For years, herbs and herbal essential oils have served well as natural ways to protect people from unwanted insects while increasing the bounty of the land. As far back as the Sumerians, a person can find historic folklore and documents that record herbal information for culinary, medicinal, commercial, and personal uses. Farmers have known that planting certain herbs among their vegetables can prevent certain fungal infections as well as insect infestations. Potpourri, while providing a fresh scent to an environment, also serves the purpose of protecting clothing from insect infestation. Rubbing certain herbs on insect bites can relieve the sting and, in some cases, reduce the swelling. Herbs used as perfume may have provided a fresh scent, but they also protected the wearer from insects and even the smells of the street. More importantly, the aroma of herbs can increase a state of well being and relaxation.

While Native Americans knew the secrets of finding the right herb or plant for the correct purpose, Europeans migrating to the United States brought with them many herbs and created herb gardens. Early housewives found pride in the selected herbs found in their gardens.

Scientific Discoveries

Today, the use of herbs or their essential oils is under scrutiny in a new venue. Scientific research is showing there is value to herbs that can be used as pesticides.

On December 20, 2004, the United States Department of Agriculture (USDA), Agricultural Research Service (ARS) issued a press release: "Turkish Plant Oils Are Lethal to Vegetable Pest." This study was conducted by scientists at ARS and at the Anadolu University in Eskisehir, Turkey, who found that Turkish medicinal herbs were toxic to turnip aphids. Turnip aphids attack collards, mustard, broccoli, cabbage, radish, tomato, and zucchini. The plants involved were species of *Bifora*, *Satureja*, and *Salvia*. The most toxic of the plants studied was the wild bishop plant (*Bifora radians*).

A more recent press release, "UBC Researcher Helps Develop Environmentally Safe Pesticides," issued by the University of British Columbia (UBC) in Vancouver, Canada, and a follow-up article published by BBC News, reported that "Herbs 'can be natural pesticides,'" on August 17, 2009. The UBC press release was issued in conjunction with research findings that were presented at the national meeting of the American Chemical Society in Washington, DC. According to both the press release and follow-up article, Dr. Murray Isman, faculty professor of Agricultural Services at UBC, has been leading a team of researchers for over seven years in researching the use of rosemary, thyme, clove, and mint for their insecticidal properties. The press release issued by UBC indicates that this "new technology destroys ants, cockroaches, dust mites, flies, wasps, hornets, and other common pests."

Natural Products on the Market

As society becomes more concerned with good food that is grown locally and as organically as possible, companies are also looking for ways to provide commercial products that can be used by farmers and home gardeners who are concerned about the impact of pesticides on the environment. This is also true for insect pests found in the home. Concern over the health of adults, children, and pets in the home is driving more people to look for ways to protect their personal space without introducing more toxins into their environment. While some people feel that using herbs is a "new technology," others have used this information for years with good results.

Farmers know that planting certain herbs with food crops provides protection from insects. When dill (*Anethum graveolens*) or fennel (*Foeniculum vulgare*) are planted in the garden, hoverflies, which kill aphids, are attracted to the area. When aromatic plants, such as rosemary (*Rosmarinus officinalis*) and thyme (*Thymus vulgaris*), are planted in the garden, they mask the smell of vegetables such as carrots. By masking the smell, the herbs actually prevent the carrot fly from attacking the carrot plant. Meanwhile, sage (*Salvia officinalis*) prevents white butterflies from attacking cabbage leaves.

This same theory can be applied to your own outdoor living space. Basil (*Ocimum basilicum*), lemon verbena (*Aloysia triphylla syn. Aloysia citriodora*), and rosemary are just some of the herbs that can be grown in pots as well as garden soil. Placing pots of these plants around your outdoor living space will deter mosquitoes and other insects. Or, perhaps you may want to think like a farmer and grow these plants in your garden.

With their insect-deterring abilities, you'll be more comfortable when you work in the garden.

If you get an insect bite, you can use crushed basil or a therapeutic grade of the essential oil lavender (*Lavandula*) to rub on the bite, which will relieve the sting and help bring down the swelling. If you're allergic to bees, you may want to plant feverfew (*Chrysanthemum parthenium; Matricaria parthenium; Tanacetum parthenium*) near your door or outdoor living space. Feverfew is an insect repellent. However, unlike other insect-repelling herbs, feverfew also repels bees. This is important to remember if you need to have the bees pollinating your garden. You don't want to plant feverfew too close to areas that need pollinating.

The house can actually be a mecca for various insects, such as ants, cockroaches, cigarette beetles, grain beetles, and insect larvae, which invade stored grains, rice, and other dried food. Cigarette beetles like to lay their eggs in clothing, especially cottons and fur covered with human perspiration, and they can be very difficult to get rid of once they invade your home. For this reason, you may prefer to protect your home and other items with herbal remedies rather than commercial petro-chemicals.

When insects invade your home, you may want to use the leaves or flowers of a particular herb. Or, you may want to create or purchase a specific essential oil. If you don't want to have leaves lying around the house, you can dry the leaves or flowers and make potpourris that can be placed in sachets. You can then put those sachets in various drawers or cupboards where you have the problems.

Potpourris and Pesticides

Basil

Basil (*Ocimum basilicum*), a staple in any garden or cook's kitchen, is used in aromatherapy and perfume; it can be quite an antiseptic. Rubbing fresh leaves on insect bites can relieve the itching, and placing pots of basil around an outdoor living space can repel mosquitoes and other insects. Basil is considered a tender annual and grows in full sun. However, you can easily start basil seeds indoors and even grow the plant in your house.

Bay

Technically, bay (*Laurus nobilis*) is not an herb; it's a shrub. Yet, this is another staple in the kitchen for people who love making soup, especially during the winter months. Bay also repels larvae and cockroaches. Just place the leaves around surfaces and floors where you find the cockroaches or use the essential oil with water in a spray bottle. If you have pets or children that like to eat anything, don't leave the bay leaves where children or pets can find them. The bay shrub grows in zones 8 to 11 in either full sun or partial shade. (Consider using lavender, too; it will do the same thing.)

Chives

Chives (*Allium schoenoprasum*) is part of the garlic family and can live on a deck even throughout the winter months. It's a beautiful plant that gets purple flowers. Yet for all of its beauty, it is a wonderful deterrent of aphids. It is also used to prevent black spot on leaves of plants. It grows in zones 3 to 9 in full sun to partial shade.

Coriander

Coriander (*Coriandrum sativum*) is better known by the name of cilantro; it's an interesting herb that is used to flavor Mexican and Indian dishes. The reason that it's interesting is that people either really enjoy the taste and flavor or find it "soapy" in their mouths. Its medicinal properties focus on infection prevention and as a digestive aid. Yet, it can also kill insect larvae that attack meats. It is a partially hardy annual that grows in full sun to partial shade.

Dill

Dill (*Anethum graveolens*) has been used for many centuries, especially in India and Europe. Some gardeners consider it a hardy annual, but it is a difficult plant to grow in warmer climates because it bolts in the hot summer sun. However, even its short life span can help plants. It is one of the herbs that attracts the hoverflies that kill aphids. (Fennel will also attract hoverflies.) Plant it in full sun.

Feverfew

Some people may not feel that feverfew (*Chrysanthemum parthenium; Matricaria parthenium; Tanacetum parthenium*) is an herb they would like to see in their gardens, because bees avoid this plant. If you have a bee allergy, you may want to plant this herb near your doors and windows so the bees don't accidentally get into your house. However, if you need bees to pollinate any flowers or vegetables, do not plant feverfew near these plants.

Lavender

There are different forms of lavender: English (*Lavandula angustifolia*), French (*Lavandula dentata*), and Spanish (*Lavandula stoechas*). All work well for potpourris as well as in essential oils for removing stings from insect bites and reducing swelling. Lavender is also effective in ridding an area of insect larvae. You can place sachets of lavender in your closet and dresser drawers to repel moths. While all the lavender plants grow in full sun, not all of them grow in the same zones. English lavender grows in zones 5 to 8. French lavender grows in zones 8 to 11, and so does Spanish lavender.

Lemon Balm

Lemon balm (*Melissa officinalis*) is used in cooking when you want to have the lemon taste without actually using a lemon. Some people feel that lemon balm has a stronger taste and actually prefer the milder lemon verbena for seasoning. For years it was grown as a plant that attracts bees. While bees are insects, the plant repels other forms of insects. Lemon balm grows in full sun to partial shade in zones 4 to 7.

Lemon Verbena

Lemon verbena (*Aloysia triphylla syn. Aloysia citriodora*) provides a lemon flavor when cooking. It also works as a calming agent. Just take either the fresh or dried leaves and rub them in your hands. For years it was used in sachets and perfumes. The use of lemon verbena in perfumes was discontinued because it causes skin sensitivity when worn in sunlight. However, lemon verbena is a wonderful insect repellent. Lemon verbena is actually a shrub that grows in full sun in zones 9 to 11, although it will grow as an annual in cooler climates.

Mint

Mint (*Mentha*) is known as an ant killer and a fly repellent. There are various mints in the Mentha family, including peppermint (*Mentha x piperita*), the most common mint known and used more often, and Corsican mint (*Mentha requienii*), which actually has the strongest mint fragrance and flavor. Not only is mint an ant and fly repellent, it is becoming one of the most common essential oils used in commercial, natural ant-killing products. Making essential oils is time consuming, so you may want to purchase the essential oil of mint. To make a repellent spray, mix about 6 drops of the oil in a spray bottle filled with water. Use the mixture to spray food counters and other places you want to protect from ants and flies. You can also place crushed leaves where you see ants. Dried mint can also be used to repel moths that can damage clothing.

Mint will grow in full sun to partial shade. However, it is very invasive. If you want to grow mint in your garden, you may actually want to plant it in a pot and place that pot in your garden to prevent it from crowding out other plants. Peppermint grows in zones 4 to 11. Corsican mint grows in zones 6 to 11.

Pennyroyal

Pennyroyal (*Mentha pulegium* in Europe; *Hedeoma pulegoiodes* in America) is also known as fleabane, tickweed, or squawmint; and while many individuals see pennyroyal as a different plant, the *Mentha pulegium* is in the mint family. Pennyroyal has been used for years as a cough remedy, and as a way to prevent moths from destroying clothing; it will also rid areas of cockroaches or ants. When using pennyroyal as an insect repellent, you can either use the fresh leaves or make an essential oil. If you use the essential oil, just put a few drops on cloth or a cotton ball and place it where there may be the potential for bug infestation. You can do the same with the leaves. Pennyroyal is a biennial plant that seems to lose its flavor after the second year. For this reason, you may want to treat it as an annual. It grows in full sun to partial shade in zones 5 to 11.

Rosemary

Rosemary (*Rosmarinus officinalis*) can be grown either as a plant or a shrub, depending on your location. As an essential oil, it can be used in bath water to relieve your aching joints after a hard day's work in the garden. It, along with thyme, also masks the scent of carrots, which deters the carrot fly. Dried Rosemary can be used as an insect repellent in your clothing closet or dresser drawer. It grows well in full sun to partial shade in zones 8 to 11. In zone 7, it can be fickle. In some gardens, rosemary becomes a wonderful shrub that lasts for years, while in other gardens it seems to last one season and die back with the first frost.

Sage

Common sage (*Salvia officinalis*) prevents white butterflies from attacking cabbage leaves. Meanwhile, pineapple sage (*Salvia elegans*) provides hummingbirds with food during their fall migration, because the red flowers are among the last to come out in the growing season. Sage likes full sun. Pineapple sage grows in zones 4 to 8 and can also be grown as an indoor plant, while common sage grows best in zones 10 to 11. It can be grown as an annual plant in cooler climates, and while it dies at first frost, it is also a prolific self-seeder.

Thyme

Thyme (*Thymus vulgaris*), along with rosemary, masks the scent of carrots and will deter the carrot fly. Dried thyme can be placed in your closet or dresser drawer to repel clothing insects. Thyme can be very fragile in rainy, humid weather, where it is susceptible to fungal infection. It grows in full sun to partial shade in zones 6 to 9. Creeping thyme (*Thymus prae-cox*) has been used in rock gardens and as a ground cover.

Conclusion

As more government agencies, universities, and chemical companies continue to conduct research on the use of herbs as pesticides, more products will surface in the marketplace. If you feel that it's easier to use those products, at least you know that you, your children, and your pets are safe.

If you can purchase the herbs or grow them, you'll find even more uses than those that have been suggested here. I enjoy sitting on my deck and not being bitten by mosquitoes. Being surrounded by herbs also has an added benefit. As the aroma of the herbs wafts through the air, my friends and I can feel the pleasant sense of relationship that comes from their wonderful scent.

Resources

Bird, Richard and Jessica Houdret. *Kitchen and Herb Gardner*. London: Lorenz Books, 2000.

Bonar, Ann. *The MacMillan Treasury of Herbs: A Complete Guide to the Cultivation and Use of Wild and Domesticated Herbs*. Houston, TX: MacMillan Publishing Company, 1985.

Brown, Alice Cooke. *Early American Herb Recipes*. Rutland, VT: Charles E. Tuttle Company, Inc., 1966.

Castleman, Michael. *The Healing Herbs: The Ultimate Guide to the Curative Power of Nature's Medicine*. Emmaus, PA: Bantum, 1991.

Erler, Catriona Tudor. *Better Homes and Gardens® Step-by-Step Herbs*. Des Moines, IA: Meredith® Books, Garden Books, 1995.

McNair, James R. and James W. Wilson (Ed.). *All About Herbs*. San Ramon, CA: Ortho Books, 1990.

Rees, Yvonne and Rosemary Titterington. *A Creative Step-by-Step Guide to Growing Herbs*. Portland, OR: Graphic Arts Center Publishing, 1995.

Online Sources

BBC News. "Herbs 'can be natural pesticides.'" http://news.bbc.co.uk/go/pr/fr/-/2/hi/science/nature/8206045.stm (accessed September 15, 2009).

Pons, Luis. "Turkish Plant Oils Are Lethal to Vegetable Pest." United States Department of Agriculture, Agricultural Research Service. http://www.ars.usda.gov/IS/pr/2004/041220.htm?pf=1 (accessed September 15, 2009).

Poon, Amy. "UBC Researcher Helps Devwelop Environmentally Safe Pesticide." University of British Columbia Public Affairs. http://www.publicaffairs.ubc.ca/media/releases/1999/mr-99-61.html (accessed September 15, 2009).

Herb
Crafts

Herb Gifts and Crafts

~ by Susan Pesznecker ~

It's always fun to make things with one's own hands, and in this piece I'll share some of my favorite craft projects featuring herbs or essential herbal oils as central features. I've tried each recipe, so you can expect fabulous results.

Before we get started, here are a few suggestions to guarantee success. Always use fresh ingredients. Collect and prepare your own herbs or find reliable resources, and choose organic providers if possible. Ask how fresh the material is before you buy. Avoid products that have been heat- or microwave-dried, as most of the essential oils will have been destroyed.

To dry herbs, pick early on a dry morning, and before using herbs for culinary purposes, soak for thirty minutes in a basin of water with a tablespoon of salt. This will cause dirt and critters to be dislodged. Rinse well, shake dry, and spread on a newspaper-lined baking sheet. Dry in a warm room—out of direct sunlight—until they feel dry and crumble easily. (For non-culinary purposes, it isn't necessary to soak the herbs.)

Store dried herbs and essential oils in a cool, dark, and dry place.

Never add essential oils to a hot mixture, unless specifically instructed, because heat causes the volatile oils to release their scent, and you'll lose the oil's "oomph."

Replace herbs after one year and essential oils after two.

Supplies Needed for the Crafts

The following list of supplies should be gathered before you begin working on the craft activities.

Cotton string

Graters: small bore, microplane, etc.

Kitchen materials: bowls, saucepans, measuring spoons, strainer

Mortar and pestle (or spice grinder)

Paper and card stock (plain index cards work well)

Paper towels

Pens and pencils in different colors

Scissors

Unbleached muslin or cheesecloth

Various sizes of glass jars with screw-top lids

Ziplock-style plastic bags

Soup Herbs

Make your friends who cook happy with gifts of herbs to add to their soups, stews, and other savory creations.

Ingredients

Assorted aromatic soup herbs: fresh or dried bay leaves, rosemary, thyme, chervil, whole allspice, peppercorns, and/or parsley. The *bouquet garni*, literally a "garnished bouquet," is a small bundle of herbs used to flavor a stock, soup, stew, braise, or roast.

Directions

To make a *bouquet garni*:

1. Assemble a bundle of soup herbs; thyme, bay, and parsley are traditional, but others are wonderful, too.

2. Tie the herbs into a small bouquet (use cotton string) or combine in an 8-inch circle of cheesecloth, gathering and tying the ends like a hobo packet. Allow fresh herbs to air dry before packing.

3. Collect the bouquets in a glass jar for storage or gifting.

4. Dry the leaves and package in a pretty glass jar.

Your favorite cook will also appreciate a gift of dried bay leaves. These are expensive when purchased in the spice aisle, but you can buy a package of fresh bay leaves for two to three dollars in your grocery's produce section.

Cocoa Kit

Chocolate comes from a seed pod but plays well with many herbs. It's recently exploded in popularity—especially the dark forms with high levels of cacao. Dark chocolate has been found to be rich in antioxidant chemicals, which repair cell damage and slow aging. High-quality chocolate makes a wonderful hot chocolate base and when herbs and spices are added.

Ingredients

2 2- to 3-ounce dark chocolate bars (60 percent cocao or higher)

A "pinch" of one or more of: red pepper flakes, dried citrus peel, ground cinnamon or cloves, dried mint leaves, or lavender blossoms

Directions

1. Pulverize herbs in a mortar and pestle if necessary.

2. Grate the chocolate and combine with choice of herbs or spices. Spoon into a small glass jar with a tight lid.

3. To use, add 1 to 2 heaping spoonfuls to a mug of hot milk; stir until dissolved. Strain if desired.

Mulling Spices

Mulling is an ancient process in which spices and herbs are infused into hot cider, juice, or spirits. Nothing says "autumn" better than a hot mug of mulled cider or wine.

Ingredients

Assorted whole spices (cinnamon sticks, allspice berries, star anise, peppercorns, cloves)

Fresh nutmeg

Fresh citrus (lemon, orange, tangerine)

Directions

1. Add an assortment of whole spices to an 8-inch circle of muslin or cheesecloth. Grate fresh nutmeg onto the mixture and add citrus peel. Tie the packet into a bundle.

2. To use, float the bundle in a kettle of simmering apple cider or red wine. Heat for 1 to 2 hours, adding brown sugar to taste.

3. You may also simply spoon whole or cracked mulling spices and citrus peels into a decorative glass jar. Add 1 to 2 heaping spoonfuls to a kettle of simmering apple cider or red wine.

4. Heat for 1 to 2 hours, adding brown sugar as desired to taste. A dollop of brandy is another excellent addition.

Decorative Gel Air Fresheners

Ingredients

Unflavored gelatin (packets)

Alcohol (vodka, Everclear, or other grain alcohol)

Essential oil (your choice)

Food coloring

Small glass jars with lids

Directions

1. Combine 1 packet of unflavored gelatin and ¾ cup boiling water; stir until the gelatin dissolves. Cool to room temperature. Stir in the alcohol and 1 teaspoon of essential oil. Add food coloring if desired, starting

with 1 or 2 drops. Divide mixture among 1 to 3 small glass jars.

2. Allow the mixture to cool completely. Once it's cooled and the gelatin has solidified, screw the lid tightly on the jar and store in the refrigerator until ready to use.

To use, remove from refrigerator, bring to room temperature, and remove lid. The room will fill with a gentle scent. The smaller the room, the better the effect.

Scented Pumice Stones

This "hard sachet" looks lovely and adds a wonderful fragrance to the room.

Materials

Small pumice stones—1 inch or less in diameter

Carrier oil: sunflower, jojoba, or apricot kernel

Essential oil (lavender, lemon, and vanilla are good options)

Shallow baking sheet

Directions

1. Heat ¾ cup carrier oil until very warm. Remove from heat; cool slightly, add 1 tablespoon of essential oil, and mix well.

2. Place the pumice stones in a bowl. Pour the warm scented oil over the stones. Stir gently to coat with oil, and allow the stones to sit in the oil for 2 to 3 hours, stirring every 15 minutes.

3. Place the stones onto the baking sheet. Allow to dry for 1 to 2 days. Strain and save the residual oil in a small glass jar.

4. Blot the stones dry and store in a lidded glass container.

To use, arrange the stones in a shallow bowl or plate; their scent will last for 3 to 4 weeks. Refresh as needed with dabs of reserved oil.

Dream Pillows

Dream pillows are designed to be placed under a pillow when sleeping. Because the herbs within are gently crushed, they release their scents and influence dreams for the better.

Materials

Two 8-inch squares of cotton or muslin fabric

Thread

Scissors

Sewing machine or hand-sewing supplies

Quilt batting or fiberfill

Two or more of: dried mugwort, lavender, spearmint, rosemary, hops, and rose petals

Directions

1. Place 8-inch squares with right sides together; sewing ¼ inch from the edge, sew along three sides.
2. Turn the pillow inside out. Cut two identical pieces of fiberfill that fit inside the pillow, and slide into place.
3. Pack about ¼ cup of mixed herbs between the fiberfill pieces, sandwich style.
4. Sew the fourth side of the pillow closed (turning the raw edges into the pillow before sewing leaves a clean edge.)

5. Place the dream pillow under your pillow or inside your pillowcase for sweet dreams!

Children's Scented Play Clay

Credit for this goes to my children's beloved preschool teacher, Eleanor Tuomi. This clay feels smooth and cool to the touch and is richly scented. It's reusable, and although not meant to be eaten, it's nontoxic.

Ingredients

Water

Table salt

Food coloring

4 cups flour

1 tablespoon alum (buy at the pharmacy)

3 tablespoons vegetable (cooking) oil

1 teaspoon essential oil (your choice—mint is nice)

Directions

1. Bring 1 cup water and 1 cup salt to a boil in a 6 to 8 quart kettle. Remove from heat and stir to dissolve as much salt as possible.

2. Cool to room temperature, then add a few drops of food coloring.

3. Add flour and alum. Mix with hands, adding additional spoonfuls of water if needed (up to ½ cup) to get the right texture. Aim for a stiff but workable dough.

4. When the flour is incorporated, poke deep holes in the dough. Pour the oils over the dough and knead in as if

you were making bread. The result should be smooth and soft, but not sticky. Add bits of water or flour if needed to correct the texture. You can also knead in additional drops of food coloring or essential oil if desired.

5. Store in plastic Ziplock-style bags (or a large, tightly-covered container) at room temperature. The clay keeps indefinitely.

Spice Necklace

This is a wonderful kids' project, but the results are fun for adults, too. Supervision is needed with children, as the project uses sharp needles.

Materials

Assorted whole spices: allspice, cinnamon, cardamom pods, star anise, stick cinnamon, whole cloves

Absorbent paper towels

Scissors or a sharp knife

Large needles

Dental floss or heavy "coating" thread or elastic thread (for stretchy jewelry)

Optional: glass, metal, or plastic beads; jewelry closures

Directions

1. Soak spices in water for about 12 hours before beginning.

2. Drain the softened spices and place on absorbent toweling. Cut the cinnamon sticks into ½ inch to 1 inch lengths.

3. Use needle and floss to string the spices and beads (if

used). Tie the ends in a square knot when finished, or add jewelry closures.

A Grow-Your-Own Kit

Anyone can grow an herb garden—create a starter kit for your favorite gardener.

Materials

Acrylic paints

3 or 4 small identical pots

Small paintbrushes

Herb seeds or starts

Tongue depressors

Permanent marker

Potting soil

Ziplock-style plastic bags

Optional: small gift tag (make these from paper and ribbon or string)

Optional: miniature garden tools

Directions

1. Use the acrylic paints to paint the flowerpots. Solid colors are fine, but if you're more artsy, add designs, patterns, etc. Allow to dry completely.

2. For each seed or start, write its name on one end of a tongue depressor. These will be stuck into each pot as garden markers.

Method one: If using seeds, create a package that includes the pots, seeds, garden markers, and a Ziplock-style bag of potting soil. Attach a "Happy Gardening" tag.

Method two: If using starts, plant in the potting soil in the small pots. Add the garden marker to each and attach directions for each herb.

Add miniature garden tools and a water sprayer if desired. These herb gardens grow well on a sunny southern windowsill and can be moved outside when the weather allows.

Moth Sachets

Looking for a nontoxic way to protect your precious woolens? Cedar and lavender are excellent at repelling moths and other pests. Try this quick project.

Materials

Unbleached muslin or cheesecloth

Cedar shavings (buy at pet store)

Dried lavender blossoms

Optional: cedar and lavender essential oils

Optional: dried wormwood

Directions

1. Cut a 12-inch circle from unbleached muslin or a triple layer of cheesecloth.

2. Pile equal amounts of shavings and herbs onto the circle. Add a few drops of essential oils if desired.

3. Gather the ends and tie into a hobo-style packet, leaving a long string on one end.

4. Hang the completed packet in a closet or tuck into a drawer.

This sachet will work for up to three months and can be untied and replenished. (Put the old contents into your compost pile.) Add wormwood to protect against silverfish.

Bath Salts

Give yourself a little pampering with some home-crafted bath salts.

Ingredients

Table or dendritic salt

Small bowl

Coarse-grained kosher salt

Epson salt

Coarse or extra-large-grained sea salt

Essential oil (lavender, mint, rosemary, and chamomile are good options)

Wide-mouthed glass jar with lid

Instructions

1. Place the table (or dendritic) salt into a small bowl. Scent the salt by drizzling with several drops of essential oil and stir well.

2. Place enough of the scented salt into a jar to fill it about ¼ of the way.

3. Add in layers of the other salts. Top with a final layer of the remaining scented table salt. The visible layers show through the glass and are very appealing.

To use, empty 1 cup of the mixture into a hot bath. To give as a gift, attach instructions and a small spoon or scoop.

Pressing Flowers and Plants

It's fun to press your own herbs and flowers and then to use them to adorn other items.

Materials

> Plant press (or use phone books, or newspaper and heavy books for weight)
>
> Acrylic spray (purchase at art store)
>
> Flowers and plant parts of your choice

A plant press is used to flatten and dry plant specimens so that they can be mounted and saved. The traditional plant press uses layers of corrugated cardboard and newsprint sandwiched between two wooden frames; the frames are tightened with a set of screws and the newsprint absorbs the moisture. Phone books, or a newspaper and several heavy books, make inexpensive replacement presses.

Instructions

1. To dry plants, cut them fresh and arrange between the phone book's pages. Arrange carefully; the way you leave them is the way they'll dry.

2. Weight the phone book down with several heavy books.

3. Check the plants weekly until dry, usually 3 to 4 weeks.

4. After use, leave the phone book open to air for several days; this dries the pages and allows you to use the book over and over.

5. Arrange the dried plants on a piece of paper. (Work outdoors—you'll need ventilation.)

6. From a distance of about 18 inches, spray a quick light acrylic mist onto the plant and paper. Allow to dry for 4 to 5 minutes, then repeat. A series of 4 or 5 light sprays will seal the plants to the paper. Spray too close or too heavily and you'll saturate the plant, causing it to weep or curl.

3. Allow to air dry for several days, until the acrylic smell dissipates.

Use this technique to create works for framing, to adorn greeting cards or notebook covers, etc.

Lemon Moisturizing Cream

Materials

Small sauce pan for melting beeswax

Grated beeswax

Petroleum jelly

Carrier oil (sunflower or jojoba)

Witch hazel

Fresh lemon juice

Borax

Lemon essential oil

Directions

1. Melt 1 tablespoon beeswax and 1½ tablespoons petroleum jelly over low heat. Slowly add 3 tablespoons warm carrier oil. Beat for 3 to 5 minutes until homogenous.

2. Combine 1 tablespoon witch hazel and 1 tablespoon strained lemon juice in a separate container. Warm gently. Stir in ⅛ teaspoon borax until dissolved.

3. Add warm lemon mixture to warm wax mixture. Beat steadily until creamy and cool, then stir in 6 drops of essential oil of lemon.

4. Spoon into small glass jars and close tightly. Label and store at room temperature for 3 to 4 weeks or in the refrigerator for up to 3 months. Can also be frozen with good results.

This cleansing cream also makes a good emollient that can also be used to soothe minor irritations, bug bites, and sunburn.

Lip Balm

Materials

3 to 6 drops essential oil (this gives the gloss its "flavor," so choose accordingly)

1 teaspoon carrier oil (sweet almond, jojoba, or sunflower)

3 drops honey

Contents of 1 vitamin E capsule (snip one end off the capsule and squeeze out the oil)

1½ teaspoons grated cocoa butter

2 teaspoons grated beeswax

Directions

1. Combine the first five ingredients over a low-heat source and warm gently, stirring to combine.

2. Stir in beeswax and blend well. Allow to cool.

3. Spoon into a small container. Use within 1 to 2 months.

Tired Foot Soak

Invigorate your "tootsies" with this soothing foot soak!

Ingredients

Dried herbs (rosemary and lavender are excellent choices)

Water

Epsom salts

Large basin

Directions

1. Add 2 tablespoons of dried herbs to 2 cups of water.

2. Bring to a boil; reduce heat and simmer for ½ hour to make a decoction.

3. Fill basin with hot water (bath temperature). Add ½ cup Epsom salts and stir to dissolve. Strain the hot decoction into the basin.

4. Test for temperature before inserting tired feet. Ahhhh . . .

Seasonal Décor from Nature

⚘ by Sally Cragin ⚘

Two centuries ago, if you walked into the kitchen of a farmhouse, you'd find herbs hanging from the rafters to dry, wood stacked by the hearth, and lavender leaves in the clothing trunk. All natural substances, and all soothing to the eye and pleasing to the nose. Fortunately, we don't live in an era where a toothache could kill us and the average female produced a dozen or more children in the course of a lifetime. However, our colonial ancestors had a lot of useful and interesting ideas about using products and objects from nature in their homes.

The following ideas range from elegant to ludicrous, and with the exception of purchasing flowers or plants, should be easy to make with what you already have in your house. You'll need some staples for decorating with herbs, including interesting colored ribbon, wire, hooks for hanging, an assortment of baskets, and raffia.

Going Natural in Winter

Ecofriendly materials are abundant in the winter season. You just need to know where to look. I was amazed to see bags of pinecones on sale at my local craft store and wondered who might buy them. A basket of pinecones on a fireplace or as a centerpiece says "holiday season," but it is so easy to actually collect these during the warmer months. Unless you're in a national forest, chances are your local park has plenty of pinecones on the ground. Add some acorns and jingle bells and you've got a basket of holiday cheer.

Helpful tip: make sure any cones or nuts are insect-free before you bring them in your house.

Red and green are the traditional Christmas colors, and you can grow your own simply by planting a holly bush in your garden (if you have a garden and live in the right zones).

Natural Ornaments

You don't have to go to special trouble—just gather twigs (or better still, have small children do so!). Make sure they're all the same length, wrap in red and green ribbon and you have natural ornaments for a tree or window.

Add other dried plants to a winter bouquet for color and interesting shapes. Dried hydrangeas and dried Queen Anne's lace still have interesting subdued colors.

Winter Spice Garland

If you have older children, or enjoy working with needle and thread, you can make a winter spice garland. You'll need star anise, popcorn, dried cranberries, and cinnamon sticks. You'll want cinnamon sticks that have completely curved to create a tube. Make a pattern by threading a star anise, then a cranberry, then a cinnamon stick, then a cranberry. One thing I learned while making beaded jewelry is that if you have "spacers," your necklace will look more professional. It's the same idea with a spice garland, and you can alternate the bigger pieces with the popcorn and cranberry.

Valentine's Day Floral Display

What to do with the beautiful heart-shaped box left over from last Valentine's Day? What about using it to make a floral display? This requires lining the old box with plastic, so the cardboard doesn't fall apart. Get enough florists' foam to fill the box, making sure the foam isn't taller than the top of the box. Dampen the foam.

You'll need flowers of different sizes, and I suggest using daisies or carnations, or a flower that fills a lot of space, and then add some smaller "accent" flowers for in-between. Cut the stems so that when you put flowers in the box, they are all be the same height. Arrange the big flowers in a heart shape and fill in the center space with smaller flowers. This makes a lovely centerpiece, and it's a calorie-free gift that is in the spirit of this special day.

Spring Festivities

Our ancestors would have beat the rugs and aired out the linens in the spring. And they would never have folded clothes without a little lavender, sage, or clover to keep things fresh. Spring decorating is the most fun, partly because the eye is craving color after winter, and the bright green of budding plants and flowers is so refreshing.

Forcing a Burst of Spring

Forsythia branches can be gathered when the buds are just visible, and they'll be very enthusiastic about flowering in a warm house no matter how deep the snow is on the ground. The "darling rosebuds of May" can be a sweet decoration, whether they are put into a small vase, or dried and then threaded into a garland or necklace.

Zen Garden

You can make a little Zen garden with a bit of green grass or moss and some small rocks or coarse gravel. You'll need a shallow container (a pie plate will do fine) to make your garden in. Begin by placing some small rocks or coarse gravel in the bottom and along the sides of the dish. Then, pry up a bit of grass sod or, better still, moss and place it on top of the rocks or gravel. Put in subdued light and keep it moist. I have a friend who makes very elaborate versions of these, using water plants from the lake nearby.

Egg-shaped Handsoap

If you want to make an interesting and useful handsoap, save all those soap slivers and keep in a jar so they're submerged in water. When you have enough to squeeze in your hands, add a scant teaspoon of coffee grounds to the mix. Shape into egg-shaped soaps, let dry and then keep by the sink to wash with and get smells (fish, onion) off your hands.

Bunny Fruit Salad

This recipe is very easy, highly decorative, and kids love it. You'll need a platter, bananas, apples, oranges, strawberries, raisins, and carrots. Peel your bananas, cut in half lengthwise. Those make the ears on your platter. Make the face shape with sliced apples arranged in a circle. The strawberry is a nose, and carrot sticks are used for the whiskers. The eyes can be raisins, and you can make the mouth with two orange crescents. Use the rest of the fruit for decoration, and if you're making this ahead of time, be sure you put lemon juice on the apple slices and banana ears to keep them from browning.

Summer Fun

Once the warm weather is underway, decorating with herbs, plants, and natural substances is very easy. You don't need much space for an herb garden, and herbs can grow despite poor soil. They do need at least 4 to 6 hours of direct sunlight a day, and moist soil, though. So, why limit your herb garden to, well, a garden? All those pretty tins that cookies or candy come in can be recycled and used to hide old flower pots. My mom is an enthusiastic collector of old boots and shoes for outdoor decorating. Every pair of canvas sneakers we wore through got new life as a holder for a spider plant.

The key to using herbs and natural substances in the summer is simplicity. The shells you picked up from the beach can have a second life if you stick one or two into houseplants.

The slow release of calcium enriches the soil. Or, use a large shell in the bathroom for a few cottonballs or lipsticks. Soap in a clamshell looks pretty, but it gets really messy very quickly.

When eating outside on the deck, you can't always count on your papergoods staying put. A collection of polished beach rocks will make wonderful weights to hold down napkins (or the edge of a tablecloth). While beach rocks are not as elegant as napkin rings, they are way more practical; plus, they don't roll away!

Quick Children's Craft Project

You can do a very fun decorating project with children if you have a good selection of clam or oyster shells. Put a couple of drops of poster paint in a primary color in the shell. Say you start with red. Have the child turn the shell so the red makes a pattern. Continue until the paint is widely dispersed. Now add a drop of yellow or blue. Children love to watch the colors start to blend, and you end up with some very cheery, psychedelic-artistic clamshells.

Independence Day Decorating

Our first-grader has been given many, many flags in the course of his life—from the mini flags that are handed out at Independence Day parades, to flags from preschool and summer camps. Around Independence Day, we take all these flags and decorate the garden and our potted plants. I remember one year, even the bird feeder got a flag! We also have a big flag, but the little ones are much more fun.

Fall Colors and Harvest Fun

Where we live in New England, there are still enough family farms so that there's a wide variety of fruits and vegetables on view. Decorating with fall produce is easy. One basic item in your decorating supply should be a cornucopia—the horn-shaped wicker basket that is featured in many Currier and Ives illustrations. Since fall colors are always bold—intense reds, crisp greens, and bright oranges—you can make a colorful centerpiece, or a decoration for an occasional table, in just minutes.

Maize is another beautiful crop that comes in during the fall. Hanging a bunch of colorful cobs on your front door, or next to your porch light, is a signal of the season.

Of course, cornhusks are an easy fall decorating choice. Start with a dozen or so, tie with twine and top with a wide, non-shiny green ribbon bow.

Vines for Fine Decorations

Using weeds and vines to create a decorator touch is easy. Gather vines before the frost sets in so they are more pliable, although vines like Virginia creeper, honeysuckle, and wisteria are very forgiving and flexible.

Start with a balloon that has been blown up to a good size. Wind your vines around the balloon and fasten with twisty-ties as needed. Weave other vines in and out. Set this aside and let it dry out. When it's completely dry, pop the balloon and you should have an interesting orb. You can also make a wreath this way, by wrapping vines around a pail or a bucket. Just slide the wreath off when you're finished.

Raffia Treasures

Raffia is an all-purpose material that can be used for winding around a wreath, or used in place of ribbon to wrap presents in brown paper. Or, you can braid a few strands together, join and tie the ends together to form a small wreath or tree ornament.

Pumpkin Fun

This year, I tried carving a pumpkin by cutting a circle in the side, rather than the top. If you try this, use a mini LED votive instead of a lit candle (LEDs are safer, too). We enjoy looking online at the creative pumpkins people make, and I'm always struck by the interesting hybrids that come along. For some years now, "ghost" pumpkins, which are nearly pure white, have been available. Next year, I'm thinking of getting some of those, and then getting a can of black poster paint and painting a couple of pumpkins black.

Every family needs a gigantic pumpkin for a jack o' lantern, but consider getting a bevy of smaller pumpkins as well. Ask if these are "sugar" pumpkins (generally, just a smaller pumpkin). Use these to decorate, and if the frost doesn't get them, you can cook the pumpkin and make pumpkin bread. I discovered that if you quarter them, seed them, and steam them, they are a huge improvement over canned pumpkin. Any pumpkin bread recipe (I use Fanny Farmer's) will make a moister, richer loaf if you're using the real thing instead of something out of a can.

Fall also brings a bounty of gourds, and every year these seem more cartoonish and surreal. We like putting a pumpkin with a little group of gourds ("the protectors" according to my son) on the steps leading up to the porch.

Halloween Scarecrow

This is a great project for kids, and it also takes care of a lot of fall leaves. You'll need a pair of old pants, an old turtleneck sweater or pullover, and a plastic shopping bag. Tie the pants cuffs closed with string or elastic. Start stuffing the pants with leaves. Tie the shirt cuffs and turtleneck top closed with string or elastic. Stuff the pullover with leaves. (You can dress the scarecrow in a flannel or crewneck shirt later if you chose to). When you're done, you should have two oddly lumpy body parts. Now, put the pants on a porch chair or lawn chair and bunch the shirt into the pants. You can make the head by stuffing the plastic bag and balancing on the shirt. Add a big hat and some old boots and you've got a scarecrow on vacation.

Putting the scarecrow on a chair makes it easier to manipulate and, if your child is of a gory state of mind, you can just stuff the pants, put them in shoes, and stick them next to the house, a la Wicked Witch of the East crushed by the house.

Crafting Essential Oils

☙ by Calantirniel ☙

I t was love at first smell when I discovered essential oils in the early 1990s. I felt like I had to have them all! Not only could I make custom blends of lovely smelling sprays, bath salts, oils, etcetera, but I liked the fact that they were plant-based, and therefore "alive." Because of this, they provided real cleansing and healing for body and soul that couldn't be duplicated with chemical fragrances. While I didn't go as far as creating a business with these products, I became quite an adept amateur, and constantly use essential oils to this day.

While some oils are rather inexpensive, such as those in the citrus family, others like rose, jasmine, and neroli (orange blossoms) are very costly. They are concentrated and worth every penny, and you would use them very sparingly. Since I have both a wonderful rose and a lilac bush, I wondered how to create my own essential oils. I found a method, but it was rather elaborate. I wanted to use a layperson's equipment, which meant that it would likely already be in my kitchen. I discovered two methods: steam distillation and pomades.

Steam Distillation

This is the method you would use for plants that have much of their scent (oils) in the leaves and stems. Plants in the mint family are a good example: rosemary, basil, and clary sage come to mind. Evergreen trees, such as pine, fir, and cedar, work well, too. Plants like parsley and geranium, and trees like eucalyptus, also fit in this category. I used this method to make a small amount of tansy (*Tanaecetum vulgare*) oil for making a spray liquid to control ants. (Don't use tansy around pregnant women, as it is a strong abortificant.) If the scent is in the flowers, make sure the steam does not destroy their scent (e.g., Lavender). If the scent is destroyed, try the second (more complicated) method.

Use a stainless steel kettle with a rounded lid and metal handle, as it will be used with the lid upside down. If your kettle doesn't have that, a stainless steel mixing bowl that is the same size as the kettle, or larger, can be used instead. You will also need a stainless steel steam basket to place on the bottom of the kettle. Add a small amount of distilled water, just enough to touch the bottom of the basket.

Place fresh plant material into the steam basket that you placed inside the kettle, concentrating it more toward the center, less on the sides. Put the lid upside down onto the kettle, and add lots of ice to the top.

Use the lowest heat possible to make steam that rises. When the steam hits the cold lid, it will condense and fall back through the plant material to become steam again. This may take some experimenting, so be patient. Periodically replace the ice in the lid (or bowl), add a small amount of water, and if you have it, add more plant material. Allow this process to happen until all plant material is exhausted, and the water is full of the essential oil, which could be an hour or two, maybe more.

Let it cool enough to handle, then using a colander that you have lined with cheesecloth (or other fabric), strain all water through the plant material while squeezing it well to get every last drop. Discard the plant material into your compost.

Find the tallest and narrowest non-plastic glass in which to put the scented water. Let it set. When the liquid cools the rest of the way, you will see the essential oil at the top of the glass—don't shake or mix. Using a glass dropper with the rubber suction device on the top, gently siphon the essential oil off the top and release into a small, clean, dark-glass bottle (amber or blue is fine). Label and enjoy! Use the water as "floral" water, or as a hydrosol for cosmetic or household use.

Pomades

While more laborious, this method can be used with plant material that would be compromised by heat and/or water.

Those include rose, gardenia, lilac, carnation, narcissus, tuberose, black locust, jasmine, and nearly every scented fruit tree blossom (e.g., peach, orange, cherry, and apple).

You will need to purchase two pieces of glass from the hardware store that will fit inside a cookie sheet and leave at least ½ to 1 inch of room all the way around to spare. Apply tape to the edges of the glass (or have the glass edges ground) to protect yourself from getting cut by sharp glass. After cleaning thoroughly, rinse the glass with water and dry. Since the top glass will be lifted often, you may want to try one of those suction-type handles to make it easier to remove the top glass.

Next, you need some kind of semi-solid fat, and plenty of it. In the past, lard was used, but if you wish to use vegetable-sourced fat, try unscented coconut oil, or (if you can find it) a vegetable-based "lard" made with sunflower oil.

When the flowers are in bloom, harvest some and gently de-petal them before placing them on the bottom glass. Place the top glass back on top. The next day, use your fingers to remove the flower petals; discard into compost. Harvest fresh flowers and repeat the process every day until you run out of flowers, or until the fat is saturated with scent. After removing the last flowers, scrape the pomade into a jar and label.

You can use pomades as they are, adding them to creams, oils, lotions, and the like. If you wish to further extract the essential oil itself, place pomade into a larger jar in which four times the amount of Everclear alcohol is added, and allow it to set for several weeks. Then, scrape off the layer of fat, and with the *bain-marie* or double-boiler method, carefully add heat to evaporate the alcohol away. Bottle the remaining essential oil in a small dark bottle.

Infused Method

If the pomade method seems too complicated, and you don't need to extract the essential oil, you can make an infused oil instead.

Get a good, scentless vegetable oil (jojoba is good).

Place flower blossoms or plant material into the oil (make sure oil covers plant material), and heat gently on a stove in a stainless steel saucepan.

You can also use a glass jar that you set on a cookie sheet and place in the oven. If you use this method, heat the oven to 150°F. Leave the oven door partially open.

Still another option is to place the flowers/plant material in a jar and pour oil to the top of the jar, covering all plant material. Place the jar in the sun during the day (take in at night) for at least two weeks. (During the waxing moon phase is the best time to do this method). Strain, label, and use!

Use and Storage

Because they are so concentrated, essential oils in most aromatherapy recipes are measured in drops, and the other base ingredients are measured in larger measures. Use a different glass dropper for each oil (available at your local drug store). The only two oils that are applied undiluted, also called "neat," are lavender and tea tree oil, and even then you will wish to use safety precautions. You will notice that essential oils are lighter than water, and even lighter than base oils (like olive, grape seed, almond, jojoba, etcetera). They tend to blend nearly right away with the oil, while they tend to separate in water, so you should shake them well before using if your recipe contains water (e.g., a room spray). A small amount of vodka or brandy can also be used to preserve your recipe, and it is best to use distilled water if at all possible. If making bath salts with sea salt, table salt, and/or Epsom salts, make sure you go light on the oils. Add them last, and use at least one-third baking soda so your salts do not dissolve until the time you intend to use them in your bath water. If you live in a humid environment, make a small amount and use it quickly.

Essential oils, whether purchased or created by you, need to be stored in a dark place in small amber or blue-colored glass bottles, and use nonmetal lids. Do not store in plastic, because the essential oils are so strong that they eat away at the plastic, suspending the chemicals of the plastic bottle into the essential oil, a rather undesired effect. If you use lids made of metals, even if they are painted, the essential oils tend to eat through the paint and into the metal. Again, this suspends the paint chemicals and the metals (many containing nickel, a common allergen) into the essential oil.

Choose lids made of hard plastic, and if possible, lined with an essential oil-resistant plastic. Using corks can be a temporary means if the oil will be used right away, but it is not recommended.

Many people who use herbal tinctures as medicine can use their old amber glass bottles to store their essential oils, and the glass dropper makes it handy to measure the oils in drops. Just boil the bottles in water for 15 to 30 minutes and dry thoroughly before use. Do not use the kind with plastic droppers.

Resources are provided below if you want to purchase bottles for storage, and further your aromatherapy education (including safety of certain plant oils). There is also information if you wish to take the next step and get special equipment that will simplify your process and increase the volume of essential oil you can make.

May all noses enjoy the true beauty of our ever-healing plant kingdom!

Resources

Rose, Jeanne. *The Aromatherapy Book: Applications and Inhalations.* Berkeley, CA: North Atlantic Books, 1992.

The Herbal Body Book: The Herbal Way to Natural Beauty & Health for Men & Women. Berkeley, CA: North Atlantic Books, 2000.

Worwood, Valerie Ann. *The Complete Book of Essential Oils & Aromatherapy.* San Rafael, CA: New World Library, 1991.

Online Resources

Both of these links have tremendous information about learning aromatherapy and essential oil distillation, as well as providing supplies.

HerbWorld's Herbal Green Pages: Bottles/Jars at http://www.herbworld.com/gp_bottles.htm.

Liberty Naturals Essential Oils. http://www.LibertyNatural.com is one of the best essential oil suppliers in the United States.

Herb History, Myth, and Lore

What is in a Botanical Name?

⤞ by Harmony Usher ⤝

Words have meaning.
Names have power.
~Author Unknown

The naming of things in the natural world is wonderful blend of science, art, and folklore. In early times, writers such as Pliny (AD 23) studied the natural world and wrote extensively about the plants that were common in his day; blending together science, philosophy, common folklore, and his own ideas without apology. Dioscordies, a Greek man who was a contemporary of Pliny, wrote extensively on the identification and use of medicinal herbs and, together with the work of

Sage
Salvia officinalis

Onion
Allium cepa

Rose
Rosaceae

Hippocrates, much of what he wrote became the basis of medical practice for centuries to come.

In more modern times, people began classifying plants in a scientific manner. Carl Linnaeus (1707–1778) developed a classification system for living organisms using two Latin names for each. Linnaeus was a traveler, a keen collector, a geologist, and a zoologist, but plant life was his deepest passion. He came from a religious family and was known to believe he was chosen by God to classify the natural world. Through his *Systema Naturae*, first published in 1735, he distinguished and named 7,700 plants.

Around the same time, an Englishman named John Ray coined the term "botany" and created rules for categorizing plants. These included English species as well as many specimens he brought from distant lands. Those interested in classifying and naming plants before him had insisted on doing so primarily by use or characterization (poisonous, good for stomach ailments, and so on) but Ray was interested in more objective qualities, such as the distinction of seeds that sprout with one leaf or two. This shift made a permanent impact on the way botanists classified and named plants.

Despite the gradual change to a more scientific method of identifying plants and herbs, many Latin and common names still give hints about the folklore or history of the plant. Many have long histories of being associated with particular attributes or folktales, and their names often reflect these beliefs.

Some of our most common herbs and native plants have fascinating histories and their names tell us much about their historic importance, role, and value. Knowing a bit about the history of both Latin and common names of our most enjoyed herbs can offer interesting insight into the long histories most of them have enjoyed and lend a richer taste to the foods we add them to.

Allium

The proper name for garlic, *Allium*, is believed to come from the Celtic word *all*, which means "pungent." Its common name is believed to have originated from the Anglo-Saxon word *gar* meaning "lance" (referring to the shape of the stem) and *leac*, which means "potherb." Garlic is also sometimes referred to as "poor man's treacle," which comes from the Greek word *theriake*. This refers to a compound used to treat against poison, and points to the medicinal aspects of garlic that were prized by many peoples around the world throughout history. The ancient Egyptians were known as "the stinking ones" because of their love of the plant, and they were known to swear oaths on bunches of garlic in the same way people might swear oaths on a holy text. It was also used as currency!

Angelica

Angelica is one of the few herbs always referred to by its Latin name only. The legend says it received a heavenly name because an angel came to a monk in the middle ages and told him that the plant could be used to cure the plague. Throughout the 1500s and right through to the time of Charles II, Angelica was thought to be an effective antidote to that horrible disease.

Coriandrum

One of the most important herbs of the East, coriander is known for both it's aromatic leaves and its sweet-peppery seeds. Despite its popularity in cooking, its name was originally derived from the Greek work *koros* meaning "bug," as it was thought to have an aroma akin to the pungent smell of the bedbug!

Laurus Nobilis

This herb, commonly known as the bay laurel, has a name history that continues to have relevance in today's culture. Its name tells us much about how highly it is regarded; the name *Laurus* comes from the Latin word meaning "to praise" and *nobilis*, means "famous" or "prized." In the past, those achieving academic successes would be given berries of the bay laurel- a "baca lauri" that now has the meaning "baccalaureate" and refers to one who has a bachelor's degree. Similarly, one is said to "rest on their laurels" when they have achieved great things and no longer need to prove their abilities. Bay laurel is an important herb in many Mediterranean countries and can be used dried or fresh. It is also a prized ornamental plant, easily lending itself to shaping and clipping, and making it popular in formal gardens.

Lavandula

Lavandula, or lavender, derives its name from the Latin word *lavendus*, which means "to be washed." This is thought to be related to the fact that the ancients of Greece and Rome used lavender to perfume their baths. It continues to be cultivated today, and its essential oils or dried flowers are used to scent soaps, lotions, and perfumes.

Melissa

Melissa is most often referred to by its common name, which is common balm and was first referred to in writing in the mid 1500s. It was highly valued by beekeepers, who would rub it on the inside of hives both to encourage the bees to stay together and to encourage new bees to join the hive. The older Greek name for this herb was *Melissophylon*, meaning "beloved by bees."

Mentha Pulegium

More commonly referred to as pennyroyal, this herb derived its name from the Latin word *pulex*, which means "a flea." This form of mint has many uses, but it is perhaps most well known for its ability to drive away fleas. It was used in its fresh and dried form in beds and sleeping quarters to keep its occupants from suffering flea bites.

Ocimum Basilicum

Sweet basil has been cultivated in Asia for about three thousand years and was used in Egypt at the time of the pharoahs. It was also grown by the ancient Greeks and spread through Rome and into England around the sixteenth century. The name *basilieus* comes from the Greek word for "king," and through the ages, basil was often referred to as the "king of herbs." Its name has sometimes been confused with the Latin word *basiliscus*—a large snakelike creature said to be able to kill someone simply by breathing on them. For generations, this contributed to a certain distrust in the herb, and spawned tales that basil could transform into flies or scorpions. These suspicions have largely shifted to appreciation over the years, and basil is now one of the most enjoyed herbs around the world.

Origanum Majorana

Sweet marjoram was prized by the ancient Greeks and its name means "joy of the mountain." Folklore tells us that it was often planted on graves, and was intended to help the dead enjoy a good sleep. Young couples were often crowned with this sweet smelling herb, which was thought to have been given its scent by Venus, who was believed to have cultivated it.

Rosmarinus

Of all the common herbs, rosemary is almost always heralded as the most "beloved," with many traditional stories associated with its cultivation and use through the years. Despite centuries of cultivation, today's varieties have changed little since its early incarnations. In folklore, rosemary has been associated with both remembrance and memory. In France, it was customary to place bunches of rosemary in the hands of the dead when they were buried, so that they would not forget their loved ones as they passed into the next world. In nineteenth-century England, it was customary for a bride to wear a garland of rosemary to signify she was taking memories of the past into her marriage. The name *Rosmarinus* means "dew of the sea," and was given to this herb because it grew most easily close to the ocean. Common folklore also stated that one could smell the scent of rosemary for miles off the coast of Spain, where it grows in thick blankets on the rocky shores.

Salvia Officinalis

More commonly referred to as sage, this herb was first grown in the Mediterranean region and is mentioned in writing as early as the early thirteenth century. Its name means "I am well" and it was believed to have many virtues, particularly with regard to its ability to promote long life. This quality was captured in the old Arabic proverb: "How shall a man die who has sage in his garden?"

Resources

Coats, Alice M. *Flowers and their Histories*. London: Hulton Press Ltd., 1968.

Small, Ernest. *Culinary Herbs*. National Research Council of Canada, 1997.

Prickly Lettuce

ᴖ by Calantirniel ᴖ

Prickly lettuce (*Lactuca serriola*, or *scariola*) and other wild species, including wild lettuce (*L. virosa*) and Canada lettuce (*L. canadensis*), are extremely plentiful "weeds" that are virtually identical to the cultivated garden lettuce (*L. sativa*) in appearance. While wild lettuces may look like garden-variety lettuce, they taste very bitter. They also have a long history of safe medicinal use. All are annual or biennial and belong in the aster family (*Asteraceae*), sometimes also called composites. Their flowers are most often yellow in color, but can be blue or other colors as well. Among other common names are bitter lettuce, horse thistle, compass plant, opium lettuce, and wild opium. If you place the Latin names in Google's image-search function, you will be able to see hundreds of photo examples, making it much easier to identify a similar species in your area.

Prickly lettuce grows on a long, sturdy central stem that is round and smooth, and the plant can grow from 3 to 8 feet tall. The alternate leaves are light green or even yellow-green, sometimes with purple spots, and they can be shaped from oval-like to serrated, where the bottoms of the leaves are often broader than the tips. When in flower, the top of the plant will display multibranched stems, with small yellow rayed flowers on the tips, similar to those of a small dandelion (*Taraxacum officinale*). These flowers, though smaller, also go to seed in a similar manner as the dandelion. The milky latex in this plant has a bitter and somewhat narcotic smell; it is, in fact, the medicinal portion of the plant.

The most telltale giveaway on how to determine prickly/wild lettuce from other plants in the aster family, besides the smell and taste of the milky latex, is that the center vein on the underside of the leaves has a row of "prickly" hair and, depending on the species, sometimes the prickly hairs appear on the outside edges, but the rest of the leaf is fairly smooth.

Prickly lettuce and the other uncultivated lettuces can be found all over Europe, Asia, northern Africa, and nearly all of North America. It grows wild along roadsides and other disturbed areas and, in many places, is regarded as a noxious weed, making it quite sustainable for medicinal use.

History and Lore

The Egyptians associated this plant with their god Min, the god of fertility, power, and agriculture. Min is also associated with the moon. He is often depicted with *L. serriola rosette*, and offerings of lettuce were made to him. Ancient Greek manuscripts referred to this magical plant as "Titan's blood" and the Romans, ranging from Augustus to Pliny the Elder, also held this medicinal plant in high regard. Strangely, the dried latex was also used to adulterate (cut) opium, which originates from poppy flowers.

Prickly lettuce is moon-ruled due to the milky substance, and it is used as a sleep/dream aid. It is coruled by Saturn, due to its chemistry being similar to henbanes.

Herbal Qualities and Medicinal Use

It is described as a sedative nervine, hypnotic, analgesic, gently laxative, expectorant, cough-suppressant, diuretic, and somewhat diaphoretic, and though it contains no opiates, it can act as a weak narcotic. Though there are many, the two most common chemical constituents are lactucopicrin and lactucin. In fact, lactucarium was a pharmaceutical available until the 1940s.

The milky latex fluid in this plant (sometimes called lettuce opium) is an effective yet mild sleeping aid, and is also an amazing pain reliever. I have personally experienced using vodka tincture for insomnia and muscle pain, and others have used it as a single remedy for a sprained ankle and gout pain relief. It was even the main ingredient in an impromptu hormonally-based migraine remedy, when other herbs (feverfew) and medicines (Tylenol, ibuprofen, and even some unknown prescriptions) did not work in the past.

Prickly lettuce has also been used to soothe chapped or sunburned skin (tea applied externally, called a fomentation); to help nursing women with lactation (internal and external use); to correct nervousness, hyperactivity, and respiratory issues (congestion, bronchitis, asthma); for acne, cough, hysteria, dropsy, digestive issues (including colic), pain/stagnation with menses, and infertility. It can even lessen (small doses) or enhance (larger doses) sex drive. It also isolates, breaks down, and moves out toxins from poisonous bites and stings. It has psychological applications for helping those with negative thinking and lack of motivation, who tend toward cold extremities and tension in neck, shoulders, and lower back. It can also help those who are overactive (e.g., teenagers with high hormonal levels). Whether overly aggressive or suffering a lack of motivation, the presence of frustration is the key.

Contraindications: According to the *Physician's Desk Reference (PDR) for Herbal Medicines*, there exist no precautions or adverse reactions with "proper" use, and it appears even to be safe for use during pregnancy and while nursing children. It is an excellent alternative for those who have salicylin allergies and cannot use willow bark, as they have issues with aspirin (salicylic acid) and its relatives. However, I do caution people not to drive after a dosage because it can cause sleepiness.

While on the topic of proper use, some people believe recreational use for the weak narcotic-type effects of prickly lettuce is worthy of pursuing. Herbalist Greg Tilford warns that achieving a so-called "high" is nearly impossible to achieve, as so much of the milky latex is needed for such an effect, and hardly worth the hassle of collection, and ingestion, for such purposes.

Harvesting to Create Herbal Medicine

Though you can harvest before a plant blooms, it is most common to harvest when the blooming season occurs, which is usually late summer to early autumn, and lasts for three weeks or more. While other parts of the plant can be used, the most common parts are the upper parts, particularly the leaves (to dry or to tincture) and the stems, including the flowers and flower buds, all of which have the milky latex substance.

The milky substance (also called lettuce opium) can be captured by cutting toward the bottom of the plant and attaching a collecting device for the juice (preferably with some protection from dirt and bugs). This juice can then be spread and dried for use by the gram. However, this is a tedious and laborious process, and for the lay herbalist, I recommend the following methods instead.

If there is an immediate need, and the plant is available and in season, use the fresh uppers—any part—to make tea. Just fill the teacup with plant material and pour boiling water over it. Then cover the cup and let the tea steep for 15 minutes. I like to squeeze the plant material to make sure as much of the milky substance is mixed into the tea as possible. The tea can be sweetened with raw honey, agave juice, stevia, or flavored with tamari sauce or liquid amino acids if you prefer a salty taste.

You can dry the leaves and flowers by gathering a bunch of plants (cut the stems long) and using a rubber band to secure the stems together. Then hang the bunch upside down in a dry place away from direct sunlight. You can also harvest the leaves and flowers themselves from the plant and lay flat (not overlapping) in a paper-lined wicker basket. The tiny insects will leave the flowers, and this can easily be separated after drying, which can take a week or so in dry areas, to about two weeks in more humid areas. I recommend keeping a heater nearby (not too close) to dry the air, which will help to avoid mold and mildew issues. If the dried herb is kept in an airtight container (I like glass jars) away from light, it should have a shelf life of two to four years.

If you prefer, you can use the stems or the entire upper plant as a vinegar or a vodka tincture. To create a vinegar tincture, place the plant material (especially stems) in a glass jar, fill to the top with Bragg's or Spectrum raw apple cider vinegar, seal, and allow to sit (even in the refrigerator) for 6 to 8 weeks. Shake the jar periodically. Filter (I use an unbleached coffee filter with a screen colander) the liquid into a glass bottle, add a label with the date made, and keep the vinegar in the refrigerator for medicinal use. This method is good for people who wish to avoid alcohol; it should last a few years.

I prefer the vodka tincture, as it is stronger medicinally, and it doesn't need refrigeration. It will also last nearly indefinitely. Again, place the harvested plant material into a glass jar, and fill to the top with vodka (40 to 50% alcohol) or brandy. Seal the jar and leave it sit on the kitchen counter for 6 to 8 weeks, shaking occasionally. Filter as for a vinegar tincture, add a label with the date made, and keep in an herbal tincture-type dark bottle with a glass dropper.

Medicinal Dosages

To use dried plant matter to make an infusion (tea), use 1 teaspoon of herbs per 8 ounces of near-boiling water, pour over and steep for 15 minutes, strain, and drink. Since it is bitter and acrid-tasting, you may wish to add some raw honey, agave juice, or stevia for sweetening, or try tamari sauce or Bragg's liquid aminos if you prefer a saltier, rather than a sweet taste. This is likely the best way if you are administering to an infant or child in which case you should use it without flavoring it. Nursing mothers can take the dosages (in any fashion) and pass it to the child through her milk.

To use the vinegar tincture, use 1 to 2 tablespoons, and ingest straight, or in water.

To use vodka tincture, use from 10 to 30 drops in some hot water to boil off some of the alcohol, and add some cold water to help you swallow the mixture.

For using either tincture (or even with plain tea), it is ideal to chase with a fruit juice or other strong and pleasant-tasting beverage. This eliminates the bitter aftertaste fairly well.

For acute conditions like headaches, menstrual cramps, pain from an injury, or insomnia, one or two doses may be enough. Make sure there is an hour or two between doses. For more chronic issues like fibromyalgic pain, acne, bronchitis, or asthma, use two to four times per day, for six days per week, as long as needed for improvement or elimination of conditions.

For external applications, use any of the above methods, unflavored, and apply to irritated areas for skin disorders ranging from burns and rashes to eczema and acne.

I hope you find prickly lettuce to be an invaluable contribution to your herbal medicine cabinet!

Resources

Tilford, Gregory L. *Edible and Medicinal Plants of the West*. Missoula, MT: Mountain Press Publishing Company, 1997.

Tilford, Gregory L. *From Earth to Herbalist: An Earth-Conscious Guide to Medicinal Plants*, Missoula, MT: Mountain Press Publishing Company, 1998.

Wood, Matthew. *The Earthwise Herbal, A Complete Guide to Old World Medicinal Plants*. Berkeley, CA: North Atlantic Books, 2008.

Internet Resources

USDA, NRCS. 2009. The Plants Database at http://plants.usda.gov.

Wild Lettuce at www.wildlettuce.com

Unraveling the History and Meaning of Names

⤜ by Chandra Moira Beal ⤛

Most backyard gardeners are introduced to plant names through labels at the nursery or garden center, or maybe through seed packets, catalogs, or books. Plants are often labeled with their common names, such as lemon verbena or St. John's wort. But plants go by another moniker: their botanical name.

Over the ages, plants have accumulated various common names in many languages on all continents. What I call mallow you may call marsh weed, or what is called mallow may be a completely different plant where you live. A botanical name is the formal, scientific name of a plant,

allium

rosemarinus

often drawn from Latin or Greek, that conforms to the International Code of Botanical Nomenclature. Botanical names refer to one and only one plant, with a few exceptions.

The huge variety of plants makes it difficult to make sense of the diversity among them. Human beings are always seeking to make sense of their surroundings, looking for recognizable patterns. Botanical names give us a universal language to describe plants that may be known by different names around the world. For the average gardener, knowing the common plant names may be enough. But for scientists and serious herbalists, more precision is required. This is where taxonomy, the science of classifying things into differing types and subtypes to make sense of the relationships between different types of plants, comes in.

Swedish botanist Carl Linnaeus (1707–78) is credited with bringing order to botanical nomenclature. Linnaeus lived during a period of intense exploration, when European scientists were discovering new plants from South America, southeast Asia, Africa, and the Middle East. This influx of new discoveries demanded organization, and in 1753 Linnaeus presented a standardized method for naming plants using a Latin binomial—or two-name—system, in which the first name represented genus, and the second, species. Linnaeus's system is based on structural differences, and has survived to present day and prevailed as the preferred method of classification.

Common names, such as valerian or Thai basil, can be easier to remember than botanical names. They are often highly descriptive and literal, taken from their purpose or growing habit, such as incense plant, soapwort, lady's mantle, or foxglove. Yet when one general name applies to many specific plants, common names can be misleading and confusing.

Familiarization with some botanical names can be a helpful tool for the gardener. The botanical name can tell you a lot about the plant, such as where it grows naturally and what it might look like. Knowing botanical names can help gardeners with their planning and maintenance chores. For instance, if you are planning a garden in a small and cramped space, a plant with "arboreum" (treelike) or "altissimum" (very tall) in its name might not be the best choice. Knowing the botanical name can help ensure you get the right plant and not end up with any surprises or disappointments (such as the misleadingly named Christmas rose, which isn't a rose at all).

Learning botanical names is easy once you get to recognize them. You'll begin to recognize root forms of words referring to varying plant characteristics, such as color, size, or shape. For example, "albus" is Latin for white, "incanus" for gray, and "lac" for milk. Any of these words may be used to describe a whitish plant suited to a moonlight garden. "Ruber" (*rubrum*), "sanguineus," "roseus," and "coccineus" all denote red.

Some names refer to special characteristics of the plants. "Pubi," "hirti," "villi," and "barbi" all suggest hairiness. *Hirtifolia* means hairy-leaved. "Barbiflora" means bearded flower. Other examples are "angustiflorus" (narrow-flowered), "cauliflorus" (flowered on the stem), and "grandiflorus" (large-flowered).

Take the example of the bluebell. In England, the botanical name for bluebell is *Hyacinthoides non-scripta*. In America, the bluebell could be both *Campanula americana* and *Campanula parryi*. In Scotland, what the English call harebells are locally known as bluebells.

Another example is sage, which has over nine hundred varieties. Sage comes in all shapes and sizes, with many different flower colors, leaf scents, shapes, and environmental tolerances. Garden sage is also known as *Salvia officinalis*. Salvia comes from the Latin *salvus* for "safe" or "unharmed," referring to its medicinal properties. *Officinalis* means "from the shop" and tells us that this plant was developed by professional herbalists. There is *Salvia farinacea—farinacea* means "mealy" and comes from the Latin word for "flour." From that we can guess that the plant has a floury look to its leaf or stem.

Many plants give us clues to their habitat in their names. *Nicotiana sylvestris* (*sylvestris* means "of woodland") tells us that this plant will thrive in dappled sunlight.

Palustris (*Caltha palustris*) means "of marshes," meaning that any plant with this in its name likes moist ground and is likely to be found growing by a stream or in a boggy area. *Littoralis*, which means "by the sea," as part of the name *Griselinia littoralis* shows that the plant is adapted to a coastal environment and can withstand salty air.

Sometimes the plant's name will say a bit about what it looks like. The addition *glauca* tells us that the plant has leaves with a gray tinge, while *lutea* tells us that it has either yellow leaves or flowers. *Icterina* also means marked with yellow (literally "jaundiced").

Some names will tell you where the plant originated. You may see *sinensis* or *chinensis* for China, *indica* for India, *novae angliae* for New England, and so on.

A botanical name can even tell you who discovered it or brought it into broader cultivation, such as *wilsonii* (Wilson), *forestii* (Forest), and *tradescantii* (Tradescant), to name but three.

Botanical Name Primer

In Linnaeus's system, the first part of a binomial plant name is the genus, and the species is the second name. It is customary to capitalize the genus and keep the species name lower case. Both names are italicized. The names are often drawn from Greek or Latin. You could think of the botanical name like your family name—your family's surname followed by your first name: Beal Chandra. "Beal" is the genus and "Chandra"is the species.

The genus is a grouping of similar species with similar characteristics. With Linnaeus's system, all organisms on earth are grouped into kingdoms, divisions, orders, families, and genera (the plural of genus). For example, the *Solanum* genus includes herbs, shrubs, trees, and vines with fourteen thousand species that share the common characteristics of being toxic, hairy plants with star- or bell-shaped flowers with five lobes whose fruit is always a berry. At the other extreme, a genus may consist of a single species, such as *Nicandra*, which shares the same flower structure as *Solanum*, but none of the other characteristics.

A genus may also be named after a person. It may get its name from its origins, or what native peoples called it where it was discovered. Most typically, the name comes from one or more of the most prominent characteristics that define the group. *Helipterum*, for example, comes from the Greek *helios* (sun) and *pteron* (wing).

Genera are also subject to change over time. As scientific research develops, some plants are split off to join other groups or form their own.

The second part of the botanical name is the species, and it is at this level that we get more specific. While the genus part of the name may or may not tell anything about the plant, the species is usually more descriptive of a particular detail or characteristic, such as color, origin, or habitat.

It may indicate the location where the species was first discovered. *Monspeliensis*, for example, means "from Montpelier." Species names may honor a person. Linnaeus is said to have named a useless weed "siegesbeckia" after Johann Siegesbeck, a critic.

There are finer divisions in Linnaeus's system, such as cultivar, variety, forms, hybrids, and subspecies that describe minor variations, but species is the level with which most average gardeners should be familiar.

Whenever you spend time around plants, get to know their botanical names. Read labels and take the time to look up their meanings. Over time you will begin to see patterns and their relationships will make sense. You'll know the difference between *Thymus serpyllum* (creeping thyme) and *Thymus pulegioides* (broad-leaved thyme) and what conditions they might need to thrive. You'll be able to shop for plants more wisely, and plan a well-informed garden space. After all, getting to know your garden friends is what it's all about.

Here is a partial list of some of the more common botanical name components that the herb gardener may encounter:

Colors of Flowers or Foliage

alba, albus—white

arg, argenteus—silvery

ater—black

aurantiaca—orange

aure, aurea, aureum—gold

azurea, azureus—azure, sky blue

caesius—blue gray

caerula—deep blue

candidus—pure white, shiny

canus—ashy gray, hoary

carneus—flesh-colored

citrinus—yellow

coeruleus—dark blue

coccineus—scarlet

concolor—one color

croceus—yellow

cruentus—bloody

discolor—two or separate colors

flava, flavum—yellow

glaucus—covered with gray bloom

griseum—gray

incanus—gray, hoary

lutea, luteus—reddish yellow

miniata—of a reddish color

nigra—black

purpurea, purpureus—purple

rosea—rose-colored

rubens, ruber—red, ruddy

rubra, rubrum—red

rufus—ruddy

sanguinea—blood-red

viridis—green

Leaf Shape

acerifolius—maplelike leaves

abr—delicate-leaved

angustifolius—narrow leaves

aquifolius—spiney leaves

buxifolius—leaves like boxwood

ilicifolius—hollylike leaves

lanceolata—lance-shaped

lauriflolius—laurel-like leaves

longifolia—long-leaved

macrophylla—large-leaved

microphylla—small-leaved

parvifolia—small-leaved

parvifolius—small leaves

palmate, palmatum—hand-shaped leaves

populifolius—poplarlike leaves

rotundifolia—round-leaved

salicifolius—willowlike leaves

Plant Peculiarities

acaulis—stemless

amabile, amabilis—beautiful

blanda—pleasant

communis—common

contorta—contorted growth habit

cordata—heart-shaped

crispa—finely waved, curled

florida, floridus—flowering

gracilis—graceful

grandiflora—large-flowered

hybridus—hybrid

incana—gray-haired

lactea—milky

laevis—smooth

maculata—spotted

majus—larger

maxima—largest

millefolium—thousand-leaved

minor, minus—smaller

minim—very small

minut, minutus—very small

mollis—soft and/or hairy

mon—one (one leaf, one flower)

multiflora—many-flowered

nitida, nitidum—shining

officinalis—used in medicine or herbalism

perenne, perennis—perennial

pictum—painted

pulchella—pretty

punctata—spotted

semperflorens—ever-blooming

sempervirens—evergreen

speciosa—showy

spectabilis—spectacular

spinosissimus—spiniest

spinosus—spiny

superbum—superb

tomentosa, tomentosum—hairy

umbellata—having flowers in umbels

variegata—variegated

villosa, villosum—softly hairy

vulgaris—common

Plant Shape

arborescens—treelike

elata—tall

elegans—elegant, slender, willowy

recta, erecta—upright, erect

fruticosa—shrublike

grand, grandi—big

humilis—low-growing

nana—dwarf, miniature

pendula—drooping, pendulous

prostrat, prostratum, procumbens—prostrate

pumilia—low-growing, dwarf

repens, reptans—creeping

scandens—climbing

Origins

aethiopium—Africa

alpin—alpine regions

andi—Andes

antill—West Indies

australis—southern

barbadensis—native to Barbados

borealis—northern

campestris—of the field or plains

canadensis—from Canada or America

canariensis—from the Canary Islands

capensis—from the Cape of Good Hope

chilensis—from Chile

chinensis—from China

europa—from Europe

hortensis—of the garden

insularis—of the island

japonica, japonicum—from Japan

littoralis—of the seashore

maritima—from near the sea

montana, montanus—from the mountains

palustris—from marshes or wetlands

riparius—of river banks

rivalis, rivularis—of brooks

saxatilis—inhabiting rocks

virginiana—from Virginia

The Poetry of Herbs

~ by Nancy V. Bennett ~

B efore the written word, poetry was used in song and story, to pass on knowledge and to inspire and amuse. In Celtic tradition, poetry was often used to explain the ritual properties of herbs, or used as invocations. But how did poetry and herbs evolve through the ages? What famous poets paid homage to the herbs we love, making them live forever in verse? Take a brief moment to reflect on the poetry of herbs.

Magic in Verse

The nine herb charm, in old Germanic tradition, is a charm set to poetry, dating from the tenth century. In a strange but elegant mixture of pagan and Christian influence, the poem tells which herbs are to be used against poison. It gives explicit instructions on the herbs, how they should be gathered and addressed, and how to prepare them.

Mugwort must be summoned by the name of una. Plantain (also known as snake weed) has to be opened from the east. Stune (another name for watercress, the herb that "grows from a stone") should be used for the poison of a serpent bite. Chamomile is most effective as a preventative herb for, according to the author:

> Remember, Chamomile, what you made known,
> what you accomplished at Alorford,
> that never a man should lose his life from infection
> after Chamomile was prepared for his food.

Weregulu (also known as nettle) helps to ease the pain that comes from being poisoned.

Chervil, fennel, lamb's cress, venom-loather (viper's bulgos), and finally, crabapple, round out the herb charm against the pox of poison. For:

> These nine have power against nine poisons.
> A worm came crawling, it killed nothing.
> For Woden took nine glory-twigs,
> He smote the adder that it flew apart into nine parts.

Not only for cures were herbs useful. An old country way to find one's beloved was to sew up a bag of yarrow and place it under your pillow. You would then dream of your beloved. The following poem is attributed to this practice, and may have started as an incantation.

Thou pretty herb of Venus's tree
thy true name it is Yarrow.
Now who my bosom friend will be
pray tell thou me to-morrow.

Bard Shakespeare, and Rosemary for Remembrance

In Shakespeare's time, herbs were symbolic as well as part of the table and medicinal fare. In *Hamlet*:

There's rosemary, that's for remembrance;
pray you, love, remember.

The tragic Ophelia, who thinks that Hamlet's madness has made him forget their love, holds out the flower to him to remind him of their engagement. Herbs and flowers follow Ophelia through the play, and the symbolism is not lost on us. Rue is for regret, pansies are for thoughts, and violets withered with her father's death.

In Shakespeare's writings, there are many herbs and flowers mentioned, so much that in the spirit of the bard, many gardeners have taken to planting herb gardens with him in mind. One of the more well known of these is the Brooklyn Botanical Gardens. Started originally in the 1920s and moved to a larger location in the 1970s, the garden hosts over eighty plants mentioned in Shakespeare's writings.

Culinary Herbs in Verse

John Milton knew that a country diet was keen to a person's emotional health. He wrote of "hearbs and other Country Messes" in his poem "The Elements of Happiness."

Poor parsley gets a bad rap in Geoffrey Chaucer's "The Canterbury Tales," for:

> *Many a Pilgrim has called down Christ's curse*
> *your parsley stuffing made them sick or worse*
> *that they had eaten with your straw fed goose*
> *for in your shop, full many a fly is loose.*

Edward Bulwer Lytton (the writer who coined the phrase "the pen is mightier than the sword,") reminds us how a meal with herbs is best prepared in his poem "Lucille."

> *Oh, better no doubt is a dinner of herbs,*
> *When season'd with love, which no rancour disturbs*
> *And sweeten'd by all that is sweetest in life*
> *Than turbot, bisque, ortolans, eaten in strife!*

Calendula and Burdock, Steadfast in Verse

Though roses have their place in poetry, another flowering herb also has inspired writers; that is the "never-wilt flower" known commonly as marigold.

George Wither dedicated an entire poem to the tough little plant, watching it as it opened and as it closed, in his poem about marigolds.

The Marigold

> *When with a serious musing I behold*
> *The grateful and obsequious marigold*
> *How duly, ev'ry morning she displays*
> *Her open breast, when Titan spreads his rays.*

Poet Robert Graves also noted the flower's returning beauty and perhaps its stubborn growing streak in his poem "Marigolds."

Marigolds

Look: the constant marigold
Springs again from hidden roots.
Baffled gardener, you behold
New beginnings and new shoots
Spring again from hidden roots.
Pull or stab or cut or burn,
They will ever yet return.

Even humble burdock has found its way into literary history, taking on an animal form, by Emily Dickinson, whose country ramblings must have made her pen the next poem.

A Burdock Clawed My Gown

A Burdock clawed my Gown
Not Burdock's blame
But mine
Who went too near
The Burdock's Den.

Other poets have also honored the herbs we love in verse, story, and song. Kipling called them "Our Fathers of Old." Emily Dickinson kept her own book, a "herbarium," with pressed flowers and herbs inside. John Keats spoke of their sweetness, Oscar Wilde of their bitterness, and how it made things whole; and like many folk of his day, Bobbie Burns lay in death strewn with "hearbs and flowers."

When you come in from your herb garden, take some time to explore another, the garden of verse.

May we continue to be inspired by both.

Herbs in Medieval Times

∗ by Nancy V. Bennett ∗

How were herbs used by our ancestors in medieval times? You might be surprised to know that herbs were often employed as a fragrant carpet, to be mixed with straw or rushes, to cover up the odors of one's hovel. Rue was used to protect one from plague, and a mixture of chicory and oil was said to make your offers irresistible to anyone downwind of you.

Not only for medicine, but in food, dyes, and rituals, herbs were part of our past. Here is a brief look at some of the ways herbs were part of history.

"Upper Crust" Herbs

For their unique tastes and scent, herbs were often used by the rich households. In their gardens, herbs such as mustard, borage and sage were grown for everyday meals, as they favored the strong flavors. Rosemary was enjoyed with a roasted pig, and its scent was said to preserve a man's youth, so some carried it with them in boxes to breathe. For special occasions, spices brought from other countries such as cinnamon, nutmeg and cardamom were added to the fare.

If you were among the very upper crust, you might be invited to enjoy a meal of "Lombardy custard" at a feast with King Richard II, a pie made with prunes, dates, figs, and bone marrow, with the addition of fresh parsley. For dessert you might be treated to a "sambocade," a medieval version of cheesecake using dried elder flowers and cottage cheese.

In the land of Baghdad, and beyond, herbs also had their place. For Muslims, a meal would not be complete without a dish known as *madi ra*, a thick stew made with mint and yogurt, onions, leeks and spices. It was a Middle Eastern equivalent of chicken soup. Herbs like thyme and coriander were used in stuffing large fish to be fried, and bread made with fresh rue leaves, pistachios, ground bay leaves, cloves, and rosebuds was a savory addition to the Armenian table.

Herbs to Heal

When the Black Death began to sweep through southern Europe in 1347, cures were useless and sometimes fatal. Bloodletting and the treating of the four humors were methods used by medieval doctors of the day. The treating of humors, or the four fluids of the body, came from the ancient Greeks. Depending on what humor was affected, doctors would prescribe purges or laxatives made by mixing herbs with drink or food, to balance out the humors. Angelica was used as a cure for patients and to protect healers from infection. Doctors would hang Angelica from their necks and chew upon it while ministering to the sick. Rue was also used as a deterrent.

Male doctors relied on knowledge handed down such as the work of Galen, a Greek physician, whose book on herbal remedies was widely used in schools. Unfortunately, his books on anatomy and surgery were also used as reference, and Galen had never seen or performed an autopsy. For those who came under the knife, the standard anesthetic was often made of potent ingredients such as hemlock, mandrake, and opium. The amounts were often incorrect, causing the patient to wake during surgery, or die before the first cut was made.

Female healers also made their mark on medieval medicine. One was a German nun called Hildegaard of Bingen, whose book, *Causes and Cures*, contained recipes for using herbs in the healing arts.

Country Herbs

Those who lived in the city had the doctors, but in the country, people had to rely on themselves. For cures for anything from acne to removing warts, a medieval woman of the day need not look any further than her own herb garden. For skin wounds, a woman might make a poultice with daisies and mint to stop the bleeding. If one's sight needed sharpening, fennel or rue would be mixed with water to make a wash for the eyes. Basil was thought to dull vision, but it was good to season pottages. Tansy would help with a pockmarked face, and betony with a sleepless night. A German housewife would mix a cream of centaury and butter to remedy the bite of a rabid dog.

If livestock took ill, a mixture of herbs was used in a vapor bath to "smoke" the animal back into health. When someone died, a garland of herbs was placed on the body to help keep it smelling fresh until the soil could be broken for its final home. These garlands were left on wooden markers once the body was buried, perhaps starting the tradition of flowers at a graveside.

A peasant's house normally was open in the day, so livestock intermingled with the home dwellers and left their droppings on the floor. The housewives would have to spread straw to absorb the mess, and as the stench was often high, herbs were also added to the mixture to disguise the smell. Lavender and rosemary were used for this, as they held up better than tender herbs, like mint. To further disguise the smell pots holding mixtures of herbs, flowers, and spices were left by the fireplace to rot. Later, someone discovered if you dried the herbs and flowers first, they were effective longer. This was the early beginnings of what we know as potpourri.

If it came to dyeing cloth or wool, herbs were also useful. Marigold, weld, or broom could be employed for a yellow tinge, and if a woman wanted to dye the gray from her hair, she would use sage.

For those who were beloved or wished to be, a nosegay of thyme, lavender, and mint was carried.

And what better way to attract a mate than with fresh, clean breath? For blushing maidens and wanting boys, wine was swished in the mouth, then swallowed. This was followed by fennel, lovage, mint, or parsley. Chewed each day, it was said to keep the mouth fresh and the teeth white.

In many ways, our herbal traditions grew from the castles and hovels of old. "Rosemary, that's for remembrance," Shakespeare wrote, and it is with great good fortune that we have history to thank for recording the many uses of herbs for the generations to come.

Highland Herbs

✺ by Ellen Evert Hopman ✺

H ere is a small selection of some plants that were used for healing and magic in the Highlands of Scotland. Using traditional plants is a great way to bond with the ancestors who will help you and inspire you in all your activities. But before you embark on the green path of the herbal healer, there are some important things you need to know.

If you have a medical condition, please consult a health practitioner before ingesting any of these plants. Modern drugs do not always interact well with plant medicines and certain conditions such as diabetes, high or low blood pressure, and pregnancy may be adversely impacted by the use of herbal medications.

To be most effective, magical and healing plants should be picked while speaking a prayer or invocation. By tradition it is best not to harvest using an iron implement (the fairies despise iron). Whenever possible, use a knife or cutting tool made with flint, bone, crystal, or stone.

Deciduous tree leaves must be harvested before Summer Solstice; after that they will contain too many alkaloids (natural plant poisons to repel insects). Always gather barks from twigs and branches, never from the trunk of a tree or you might kill the tree. The medicinal properties of trees are also found in the thin living layer of tissue, just under the bark, called the cambium. The bark of the root also has medicinal properties.

Roots are gathered in the very early spring or in the fall after the plant begins to die back. Gather flowers just as they begin to open.

All doses indicated below assume a 150-pound adult is taking the herbal brew. A 75-pound child would get half the dose and so on. (Adjust amounts according to body weight.) Infants can get the benefit of herbs via their mother's breast milk (the mother should take the usual adult dose.)

Please use only organic herbs, as commercially harvested herbs contain too much pesticide and always prepare the teas in a non-aluminum pot with a tight lid (volatile oils are lost via the steam). As a general rule, roots, barks, and berries are simmered (decocted) and leaves and flowers are steeped (infused) for about 20 minutes. Herbal teas can be kept for up to a week in a glass jar with a tight lid, in the refrigerator.

Herbal brews are generally most effective when taken in small doses throughout the day and not with meals.

Poultices are made by putting plants in a blender with a little water, pouring the liquid into a bowl, and adding powdered slippery elm bark or buckwheat flour (don't use wheat, as many are allergic to it) to reach a "pie dough" consistency. Roll the poultice out on a clean cloth with a rolling pin and apply the "pancake" to a burn, sprain, wound, or skin irritation, for 1 hour. Remove and discard.

Salves are made by gently simmering herbs in butter or virgin cold-pressed olive oil (traditional Scottish healers use butter or lard) and adding hot, melted beeswax. Use 3 or 4 tablespoons of hot melted beeswax for every cup of oil used. The oil and beeswax must be simmering hot when combined or the salve won't harden. Strain and put into very clean glass jars.

When harvesting plant medicines, the following rule applies: "Walk by the first seven, leave the eighth for the animals, you may take the ninth." Do not gather a plant if there are less than nine plants left. Be sure to research which species are endangered in your area and try to help the species you harvest by replanting seeds, only taking a section of root and replanting the rest, etc. Think in terms of the next seven generations each time you gather medicinal and food plants. When in doubt, don't pick.

Bog Violet, Butterwort, Marsh Violet

Parts used: the leaves

Gaelic: *móthan*

Latin: *Pinguicula vulgaris*

The leaves are used to poultice sores and chapped hands. The leaves are antispasmodic and antitussive and have been used to make a cough remedy for whooping cough. Gather the leaves in early summer just as the plant comes into flower and dry for use throughout the year.

Lore

This most magical of Highland plants is worn in a golden amulet or as a charm to ward off evil and misfortune including unrequited love, starvation, drowning, and the loss of a court case.

To make a love spell, a woman kneels on her left knee and gathers nine roots, knotting them together to make a *cuach* or ring. The woman puts the ring into the mouth of a girl who is seeking a lover, in the name of the sun, moon, and stars, and of the Three Worlds. When the girl meets the man she desires, she places the ring into her mouth. Should the man kiss her while the ring is in her mouth, he will be bound to her forever. *Móthan* is put under a woman in labor to ensure safe delivery and is carried by travelers as protection. It can be secretly sewn into one's clothing (women sew it into their bodice; men put it under their left arm).

Feed the herb to an animal such as a goat or cow and drink its milk to gain magical protection. Place it under the churn or milk pail to prevent fairies and sorcerers from stealing the milk. Weave a hoop of milkwort (*Polygala vulgaris*), butterwort, dandelion (*Taraxacum spp.*), and marigold (*Calendula officinalis*) and bind it with three threads made from fairy flax (*Linum catharticum*). Then place it under the milk bucket to stop witches and sorcerers from stealing the milk.

Elder, Bourtree

Parts used: the roots, bark, young shoots, leaves, flowers, fruits

Gaelic: *ruis*

Latin: *Sambucus nigra*

Elder flower water is used to wash the face as a skin tonic. Elder flowers, pollen, almond oil, and lard are used to make a healing salve for dry, flaky skin conditions. The flower tea opens skin pores and promotes sweating, making it helpful for fevers and rheumatism.

The young leaves (the leaves should be gathered before Summer Solstice) are used in salves for wounds and burns. The tea of the young leaves and shoots increases urine production and helps edema.

The bark and root are emetic and diuretic and must be used fresh. Caution: large doses of the bark and root can lead to inflammation of the bowels and violent purging.

The berry tea and wine are rich in iron, building to the blood, and a remedy for bronchitis, asthma, flu, and chest colds. The berries should be cooked before eating or juicing. They can be made into a mildly laxative jam that will soothe intestinal irritations.

Elderberries can be baked into pies, scones, and breads.

Recipe for Bark or Root Bark Tea

1 teaspoon fresh bark, or root bark steeped in ½ cup boiled water.

Take ¼ cup four times a day and no more (see caution above).

Flower Tea

2 teaspoons of flowers per 1 cup of water

Steep flowers in hot water; take hot up to 3 cups a day. The flower tea is safe for children and babies to relieve fever.

Lore

Elder protects against sorcery. Whip handles for hearse drivers were once made of elder to guard against ghosts. It is very unlucky to cut one down, or burn its wood.

Dried elderberries picked on Midsummer's Day can be placed on the windowsill to prevent evil from entering. As with rowan, an elder cross is protective of the house and barn.

The juice of the inner bark is applied to the eyelids to give someone "the sight."

Stand or sleep under an elder on Samhain or Beltane Eve and you will see fairies.

Wear a sprig somewhere on your person to ward off evil spirits.

Due to its healing virtues, this plant is said to have a strong female Spirit that inhabits it, known as the Elder Mother.

Hawthorn, May Tree, Whitethorn

Parts used: flowers, leaves, and fruits

Gaelic: *sgiach, sgitheach*

Latin: *Crataegus monogyna, Crataegus oxyacantha*

Steep the flower buds and young leaves to make a tea for sore throats. Tincture the flowers and leaves in early spring or the red berries in the fall to make a heart tonic that will help to balance blood pressure. Caution: this herb lowers blood pressure over time. The berries can also be simmered to make a sore throat tea.

Flower tea: steep 2 teaspoons buds per 1 cup of water; take up to 1½ cups a day in ¼ cup doses. Berry tea: simmer 1 teaspoon crushed berries per ½ cup water for about 20 minutes. Take up to 1½ cups a day in ¼ cup doses.

Lore

The totem plant of the Ogilvies. Where oak and ash and thorn grow together, one is likely to see fairies.

Hazel

Parts used: the nuts

Gaelic: *calltainn*

Latin: *Corylus avellana*

An important food in ancient times and thus given many mystical associations. Hazelnuts are a rich source of carbohydrates, protein, phosphorus, magnesium, potassium, copper, and fatty acids. The powdered nuts are mixed with mead or honey water to help ease chronic coughs. Add pepper (*Piper nigrum*) to the drink to help draw mucus from the sinus passages.

The dried and powdered husks and shells are simmered in red wine to help stop diarrhea.

Hazelnut milk is given to sick children and to those who can't tolerate cow's milk. Soak the fresh nuts in water overnight and blend.

Hazel rods are cut on Midsummer's Day to be used for dowsing and water-witching, and to find veins of gold, coal, or lead, and to find lost or hidden objects. If two nuts are found in one shell it is very unlucky to eat them. Hazelnuts are sacred to goddesses because of the milk in the green nut, and because hazelnut milk is given to sick children. Hazel is associated with the gods of thunder, fire, and lightning, because its wood is used to make fires by friction. The Salmon of Wisdom eat the nuts that fall from nine magical hazels into the well of Segais, or Connla's well, the source of all inspiration and knowledge. For every nut they eat, the salmon get a spot (possibly a reference to an ancient system of initiation). Any person who eats of the salmon becomes at once a seer or a poet.

Heather

Parts used: the flowering herb, fresh or dried

Gaelic: *fraoch*

Latin: *Calluna vulgaris, Erica cinerea, Erica tetralix*

Heather tea is soothing to the nerves and promotes sleep. Apply as a poultice or compress to the head for headache or insomnia, stuff pillows and mattresses with it to obtain restful sleep.

A decoction of the flowering tops helps chest conditions and coughs. The tea benefits indigestion, cystitis, diarrhea, and hay fever, and has been used for coughs, nervous conditions, depression, gout, rheumatic pains, and heart complaints. The tea helps nursing mothers increase breast milk.

Heather liniments are applied to arthritis and rheumatism and a hot poultice of the flowers is applied to chilblains. Heather is slightly diuretic and antimicrobial. It strengthens the heart and slightly raises blood pressure. Steep 1 teaspoon shoots per ½ cup freshly boiled water or simmer 4 teaspoon shoots per ½ cup water for 5 minutes. Take ¼ cup twice a day.

Lore

The Picts are said to have made ale from heather, without the use of hops. Here is a recipe from Wilma Paterson of the Isle of Skye.

Recipe for Ale

1 gallon heather tops

2 pounds malt extract

1.5 pounds sugar (or 1 pound honey)

3 gallons water

1 ounce yeast

1. Cut the heather when it first comes into bloom; simmer in 1 gallon of water for about 1 hour.

2. Strain through a jelly bag onto the sweetener and the malt extract; stir until dissolved.

3. Add the remaining water and when lukewarm, the yeast.

White heather is especially magical and brings good luck. It grows only on the grave of a fairy, or on ground where no blood has ever been shed. Heather tops should be gathered at dawn for greatest magical potency.

Ivy and English Ivy

Parts used: the leaf and twigs

Gaelic: *eidheann*

Latin: *Hedera helix*

Tincture the leaves in vinegar to treat corns; add the leaves to burn salves. Simmer the leaves in water to make a wash for ulcers, wounds, burns, boils, dandruff, and skin irritations, using about 1 teaspoon herb per cup of water. The twigs are simmered in butter to make a sunburn salve.

Caution: This plant causes contact dermatitis in some individuals. It is for external use only.

Lore

On the eve of a Fire festival (Samhain, Imbolc, Beltane, Lugnasadh) pin three leaves of ivy onto your nightgown to dream of your future lover. Bind ivy, woodbine or bramble, and rowan into a wreath and hang it over the house or barn to bring protection from witchcraft, the evil eye, and cattle diseases. Make a wreath of milkwort, butterwort, dandelion, and marigold, and bind it with a triple cord. Place it under the milk pail to prevent the milk from being charmed away.

Juniper, or Mountain Yew

Parts used: the dried, ripe berries

Gaelic: *samhan, aiteann*

Latin: *Juniperus communis*

The berries are used to flavor drinks, as a poultice for snake bite, and in massage oils for rheumatism and arthritis.

A tea of the berries is said to benefit chest congestion and relieve edema resulting from heart, kidney, or liver disease. The berries are a urinary antiseptic that is useful for cystitis, suppression of urine, and catarrh of the bladder. The berry tea helps weak digestion and gas.

Caution: The berries are emmenagogue and should be avoided by pregnant women. Do not take the tea for more than two weeks, because it can cause kidney irritation.

Recipe for Tea

Use 1 teaspoon crushed berries per ½ cup water; steep for 10 minutes. Take ¼ cup two or four times per day.

Lore

Burn juniper branches before the entrance to the house and barn on New Year's morning as an act of ritual purification. To work magically, the plant must be pulled out by the roots, the branches tied into four bundles and taken between five fingers, while chanting a prayer.

Mint

Parts used: the herb as it comes into bloom

Gaelic: *meant*

Latin: *Mentha spp.*

Mint is a popular beverage tea that improves digestion and dispels gas.

For pains in the side after jaundice, combine mint, bog-bean (*Menyanthes trifoliata*), and raspberry (*Rubus spp.*).

Add mint and lemon balm (*Melissa officinalis*) to the bath to heal nerves and sinews.

Mint can be used to poultice bee and wasp stings.

The tea makes a gargle for mouth sores and sore gums.

A strong tea of spearmint (*Mentha spicata*) can be used to bathe chapped hands, and for fevers.

To soothe flu and to ward off a cold, combine peppermint (*Mentha piperita*) with elder flowers (*Sambucus nigra*) and yarrow (*Achillea millefolium*) or boneset (*Eupatorium perfoliatum*).

For abdominal cramps, diarrhea, and nausea, take the hot tea in milk or water.

Peppermint eases heart palpitations.

For nervous problems, combine peppermint with wood betony (*Stachys officinalis*) as a tea.

Recipe for Soothing Teething Tea

Combine:

> ½ ounce mint
>
> ½ ounce skullcap (*Scutellaria lateriflora*)
>
> ½ ounce pennyroyal (*Mentha pulegium*)

1. Steep for 30 minutes in a pint of freshly boiled water.

2. Sweeten and give to the child in teaspoon doses.

Recipe for Mint Tea

Add 2 to 3 teaspoon mint leaves per 1 cup of water. Take 1 to 2 cups a day for no more than eight days. Then stop for a week.

Senna (*Cassia spp.*), mint (*Mentha spp.*), and rue (*Ruta graveolens*) are plaited and worn as a bracelet to repel evil. Scatter mint leaves around food to deter mice, which loathe the smell. Oil of peppermint is repulsive to rats.

In my personal experience, mint is a wonderful motivator that attracts success with finances and other projects. Add the oil to shampoos, soaps, and bath water.

Rowan, European Mountain Ash

Parts used: the berries

Gaelic: *caorann*

Latin: *Sorbus aucuparia*

Note: *Sorbus americana*, American mountain ash, has identical properties and orange berries

The juice of the ripe red berries is laxative and makes a gargle for sore throats. Simmer the berries and strain the liquid to make a gargle for tonsillitis that is rich in vitamin C. Once cooked, the berries become astringent. In the Highlands, a syrup is made with rowan berries, honey, and apples to treat colds. The berries are made into a jam that benefits diarrhea and is safe for young children.

Rowan Berry Jam

1 part ripe berries (gather after the first frost)

½ part sugar or ¼ part honey

1 part apples

Take 1 tablespoon of the jam, 3 to 5 times a day, for diarrhea in adults and children.

Juice

One teaspoon fresh berry juice can be taken in water.

Dried Berries

Soak 1 teaspoon dried berries per 1 cup of water for 10 hours and take ¼ cup, 4 times a day.

Lore

Possibly the most ubiquitous magical plant of the Highlands, every homeowner once strove to have a rowan tree nearby. Twigs, wreaths, and crosses of rowan were placed in the home and barn as protective charms. Furniture, cradles, boats, tools, carts, and houses were made of rowan wood to bring luck and protection from evil sorcery.

> *The Hags came back, finding their charms,*
> *Most powerfully withstood,*
> *For Warlocks, Witches cannot work,*
> *Where there is rowan tree wood.*
>
> ("The Laidley Worm," traditional)

Rowan twigs bound with red thread were tied to an animal's tail to protect it from the evil eye.

Put a sprig of rowan on your hat for luck or sew a tiny equal-armed solar cross of rowan, bound with red thread, into your clothing. Carry rowan to ward off rheumatism.

Rowan berries are said to be the food of the Tuatha Dé Danann (the fairies), which is why rowans are seen near stone cairns and circles. Rowan wood was once used to make the crossbeam in the chimney called the *rantree* (rowan tree). The churn staffs, the distaff of the loom, the pin of the plow, and parts of the watermill were all made from rowan to bring magical aid and protection. Rowan was planted near the door and trained to grow in an arch over the barn door or the farm gate to keep evil from entering. At the fire festivals, a rowan wand was placed on all the door lintels and a piece in every pocket. Rowan wood was used to build the ritual fires upon which bannocks were baked on holy days. Coffins were made of rowan wood to prevent the dead from returning to haunt the living.

Resources

Bartram, Thomas. *Bartram's Encyclopedia of Herbal Medicine*, New York: Marlowe and Company, 1998.

Beith, Mary. *Healing Threads*. Edinburgh: Polygon, 1995.

Foster, Steven and James A. Duke. *Eastern/Central Medicinal Plants*. New York and Boston: Houghton Mifflin, 1990.

Grieve, M. *A Modern Herbal, Vol. I, II*. New York: Dover Publications, 1971.

Hopman, Ellen Evert, *A Druid's Herbal of Sacred Tree Medicine*, Rochester, VT: Destiny Books, 2008.

———. *A Druids Herbal: For the Sacred Earth Year*, Rochester, VT: Destiny Books, 1995.

Hopman, Ellen Evert. *Tree Medicine-Tree Magic*, Custer, WA: Phoenix Publishing Inc., 1991.

Livingstone, Sheila. *Scottish Customs*. New York: Barnes and Noble Books, 1997.

Lust, John. *The Herb Book*. New York: Bantam Books, 1974.

Marwick, Ernest. *The Folklore of Orkney and Shetland*. Edinburgh: Birlinn Ltd., 2005.

McNeill, F. Marian. *The Silver Bough, Vol. I*, Glascow, Scotland: MacLellan, 1977.

Miller, Joyce. *Magic and Witchcraft in Scotland*. Mussepoundurgh, Scotland: Goblinshead, 2005.

Potterton, David, ed. *Culpepper's Color Herbal*. New York: Sterling Publishing Co. Inc., 1983.

Moon Signs, Phases, and Tables

The Quarters and Signs
of the Moon

Everyone has seen the moon wax and wane through a period of approximately twenty-nine-and-a-half days. This circuit from new moon to full moon and back again is called the lunation cycle. The cycle is divided into parts called quarters or phases. There are several methods by which this can be done, and the system used in the *Herbal Almanac* may not correspond to those used in other almanacs.

The Quarters
First Quarter

The first quarter begins at the new moon, when the sun and moon are in the same place, or conjunct. (This means that the sun and moon are in the same degree of the same sign.) The moon is not visible at first, since it rises at the same time as the sun. The new moon is the time of new beginnings, beginnings of projects that favor growth, externalization of activities, and the growth of ideas. The first quarter is the time of germination, emergence, beginnings, and outwardly directed activity.

Second Quarter

The second quarter begins halfway between the new moon and the full moon, when the sun and moon are at right angles, or a ninety-degree square, to each other. This half moon rises around noon and sets around midnight, so it can be seen in the western sky during the first half of the night. The second quarter is the time of growth and articulation of things that already exist.

Third Quarter

The third quarter begins at the full moon, when the sun and moon are opposite one another and the full light of the sun can shine on the full sphere of the moon. The round moon can be seen rising in the east at sunset, and then rising a little later each evening. The full moon stands for illumination, fulfillment, culmination, completion, drawing inward, unrest, emotional expressions, and hasty actions leading to failure. The third quarter is a time of maturity, fruition, and the assumption of the full form of expression.

Fourth Quarter

The fourth quarter begins about halfway between the full moon and new moon, when the sun and moon are again at ninety degrees, or square. This decreasing moon rises at midnight and can be seen in the east during the last half of the night, reaching the overhead position just about as the sun rises. The fourth quarter is a time of disintegration and drawing back for reorganization and reflection.

The Signs

Moon in Aries

Moon in Aries is good for starting things, but lacking in staying power. Things occur rapidly, but also quickly pass.

Moon in Taurus

With moon in Taurus, things begun during this sign last the longest and tend to increase in value. Things begun now become habitual and hard to alter.

Moon in Gemini

Moon in Gemini is an inconsistent position for the moon, characterized by a lot of talk. Things begun now are easily changed by outside influences.

Moon in Cancer

Moon in Cancer stimulates emotional rapport between people. It pinpoints need and supports growth and nurturance.

Moon in Leo

Moon in Leo accents showmanship, being seen, drama, recreation, and happy pursuits. It may be concerned with praise and subject to flattery.

Moon in Virgo

Moon in Virgo favors accomplishment of details and commands from higher up, while discouraging independent thinking.

Moon in Libra

Moon in Libra increases self-awareness. This moon favors self-examination and interaction with others, but discourages spontaneous initiative.

Moon in Scorpio

Moon in Scorpio increases awareness of psychic power. It precipitates psychic crises and ends connections thoroughly.

Moon in Sagittarius

Moon in Sagittarius encourages expansionary flights of imagination and confidence in the flow of life.

Moon in Capricorn

Moon in Capricorn increases awareness of the need for structure, discipline, and organization. Institutional activities are favored.

Moon in Aquarius

Moon in Aquarius favors activities that are unique and individualistic, concern for humanitarian needs and society as a whole, and improvements that can be made.

Moon in Pisces

During moon in Pisces, energy withdraws from the surface of life and hibernates within, secretly reorganizing and realigning.

January Moon Table

Date	Sign	Element	Nature	Phase
1 Sat	Sagittarius	Fire	Barren	4th
2 Sun	Sagittarius	Fire	Barren	4th
3 Mon 2:39 am	Capricorn	Earth	Semi-fruitful	4th
4 Tue	Capricorn	Earth	Semi-fruitful	New 4:03 am
5 Wed 11:08 am	Aquarius	Air	Barren	1st
6 Thu	Aquarius	Air	Barren	1st
7 Fri 9:57 pm	Pisces	Water	Fruitful	1st
8 Sat	Pisces	Water	Fruitful	1st
9 Sun	Pisces	Water	Fruitful	1st
10 Mon 10:24 am	Aries	Fire	Barren	1st
11 Tue	Aries	Fire	Barren	1st
12 Wed 10:37 pm	Taurus	Earth	Semi-fruitful	2nd 6:31 am
13 Thu	Taurus	Earth	Semi-fruitful	2nd
14 Fri	Taurus	Earth	Semi-fruitful	2nd
15 Sat 8:23 am	Gemini	Air	Barren	2nd
16 Sun	Gemini	Air	Barren	2nd
17 Mon 2:29 pm	Cancer	Water	Fruitful	2nd
18 Tue	Cancer	Water	Fruitful	2nd
19 Wed 5:16 pm	Leo	Fire	Barren	Full 4:21 pm
20 Thu	Leo	Fire	Barren	3rd
21 Fri 6:10 pm	Virgo	Earth	Barren	3rd
22 Sat	Virgo	Earth	Barren	3rd
23 Sun 6:59 pm	Libra	Air	Semi-fruitful	3rd
24 Mon	Libra	Air	Semi-fruitful	3rd
25 Tue 9:15 pm	Scorpio	Water	Fruitful	3rd
26 Wed	Scorpio	Water	Fruitful	4th 7:57 am
27 Thu	Scorpio	Water	Fruitful	4th
28 Fri 1:55 am	Sagittarius	Fire	Barren	4th
29 Sat	Sagittarius	Fire	Barren	4th
30 Sun 9:04 am	Capricorn	Earth	Semi-fruitful	4th
31 Mon	Capricorn	Earth	Semi-fruitful	4th

February Moon Table

Date	Sign	Element	Nature	Phase
1 Tue 6:21 pm	Aquarius	Air	Barren	4th
2 Wed	Aquarius	Air	Barren	New 9:31 pm
3 Thu	Aquarius	Air	Barren	1st
4 Fri 5:24 am	Pisces	Water	Fruitful	1st
5 Sat	Pisces	Water	Fruitful	1st
6 Sun 5:45 pm	Aries	Fire	Barren	1st
7 Mon	Aries	Fire	Barren	1st
8 Tue	Aries	Fire	Barren	1st
9 Wed 6:22 am	Taurus	Earth	Semi-fruitful	1st
10 Thu	Taurus	Earth	Semi-fruitful	1st
11 Fri 5:20 pm	Gemini	Air	Barren	2nd 2:18 am
12 Sat	Gemini	Air	Barren	2nd
13 Sun	Gemini	Air	Barren	2nd
14 Mon 12:48 am	Cancer	Water	Fruitful	2nd
15 Tue	Cancer	Water	Fruitful	2nd
16 Wed 4:14 am	Leo	Fire	Barren	2nd
17 Thu	Leo	Fire	Barren	2nd
18 Fri 4:39 am	Virgo	Earth	Barren	Full 3:36 am
19 Sat	Virgo	Earth	Barren	3rd
20 Sun 4:01 am	Libra	Air	Semi-fruitful	3rd
21 Mon	Libra	Air	Semi-fruitful	3rd
22 Tue 4:29 am	Scorpio	Water	Fruitful	3rd
23 Wed	Scorpio	Water	Fruitful	3rd
24 Thu 7:46 am	Sagittarius	Fire	Barren	4th 6:26 pm
25 Fri	Sagittarius	Fire	Barren	4th
26 Sat 2:32 pm	Capricorn	Earth	Semi-fruitful	4th
27 Sun	Capricorn	Earth	Semi-fruitful	4th
28 Mon	Capricorn	Earth	Semi-fruitful	4th

March Moon Table

Date	Sign	Element	Nature	Phase
1 Tue 12:14 am	Aquarius	Air	Barren	4th
2 Wed	Aquarius	Air	Barren	4th
3 Thu 11:47 am	Pisces	Water	Fruitful	4th
4 Fri	Pisces	Water	Fruitful	New 3:46 pm
5 Sat	Pisces	Water	Fruitful	1st
6 Sun 12:14 am	Aries	Fire	Barren	1st
7 Mon	Aries	Fire	Barren	1st
8 Tue 12:52 pm	Taurus	Earth	Semi-fruitful	1st
9 Wed	Taurus	Earth	Semi-fruitful	1st
10 Thu	Taurus	Earth	Semi-fruitful	1st
11 Fri 12:31 am	Gemini	Air	Barren	1st
12 Sat	Gemini	Air	Barren	2nd 6:45 pm
13 Sun 10:29 am	Cancer	Water	Fruitful	2nd
14 Mon	Cancer	Water	Fruitful	2nd
15 Tue 3:33 pm	Leo	Fire	Barren	2nd
16 Wed	Leo	Fire	Barren	2nd
17 Thu 4:53 pm	Virgo	Earth	Barren	2nd
18 Fri	Virgo	Earth	Barren	2nd
19 Sat 4:03 pm	Libra	Air	Semi-fruitful	Full 2:10 pm
20 Sun	Libra	Air	Semi-fruitful	3rd
21 Mon 3:17 pm	Scorpio	Water	Fruitful	3rd
22 Tue	Scorpio	Water	Fruitful	3rd
23 Wed 4:45 pm	Sagittarius	Fire	Barren	3rd
24 Thu	Sagittarius	Fire	Barren	3rd
25 Fri 9:57 pm	Capricorn	Earth	Semi-fruitful	3rd
26 Sat	Capricorn	Earth	Semi-fruitful	4th 8:07 am
27 Sun	Capricorn	Earth	Semi-fruitful	4th
28 Mon 7:00 am	Aquarius	Air	Barren	4th
29 Tue	Aquarius	Air	Barren	4th
30 Wed 6:38 pm	Pisces	Water	Fruitful	4th
31 Thu	Pisces	Water	Fruitful	4th

April Moon Table

Date	Sign	Element	Nature	Phase
1 Fri	Pisces	Water	Fruitful	4th
2 Sat 7:16 am	Aries	Fire	Barren	4th
3 Sun	Aries	Fire	Barren	New 10:32 am
4 Mon 7:46 pm	Taurus	Earth	Semi-fruitful	1st
5 Tue	Taurus	Earth	Semi-fruitful	1st
6 Wed	Taurus	Earth	Semi-fruitful	1st
7 Thu 7:22 am	Gemini	Air	Barren	1st
8 Fri	Gemini	Air	Barren	1st
9 Sat 5:02 pm	Cancer	Water	Fruitful	1st
10 Sun	Cancer	Water	Fruitful	1st
11 Mon 11:37 pm	Leo	Fire	Barren	2nd 8:05 am
12 Tue	Leo	Fire	Barren	2nd
13 Wed	Leo	Fire	Barren	2nd
14 Thu 2:40 am	Virgo	Earth	Barren	2nd
15 Fri	Virgo	Earth	Barren	2nd
16 Sat 2:59 am	Libra	Air	Semi-fruitful	2nd
17 Sun	Libra	Air	Semi-fruitful	Full 10:44 pm
18 Mon 2:19 am	Scorpio	Water	Fruitful	3rd
19 Tue	Scorpio	Water	Fruitful	3rd
20 Wed 2:50 am	Sagittarius	Fire	Barren	3rd
21 Thu	Sagittarius	Fire	Barren	3rd
22 Fri 6:24 am	Capricorn	Earth	Semi-fruitful	3rd
23 Sat	Capricorn	Earth	Semi-fruitful	3rd
24 Sun 1:59 pm	Aquarius	Air	Barren	4th 10:47 pm
25 Mon	Aquarius	Air	Barren	4th
26 Tue	Aquarius	Air	Barren	4th
27 Wed 12:57 am	Pisces	Water	Fruitful	4th
28 Thu	Pisces	Water	Fruitful	4th
29 Fri 1:33 pm	Aries	Fire	Barren	4th
30 Sat	Aries	Fire	Barren	4th

May Moon Table

Date	Sign	Element	Nature	Phase
1 Sun	Aries	Fire	Barren	4th
2 Mon 1:58 am	Taurus	Earth	Semi-fruitful	4th
3 Tue	Taurus	Earth	Semi-fruitful	New 2:51 am
4 Wed 1:09 pm	Gemini	Air	Barren	1st
5 Thu	Gemini	Air	Barren	1st
6 Fri 10:32 pm	Cancer	Water	Fruitful	1st
7 Sat	Cancer	Water	Fruitful	1st
8 Sun	Cancer	Water	Fruitful	1st
9 Mon 5:35 am	Leo	Fire	Barren	1st
10 Tue	Leo	Fire	Barren	2nd 4:33 pm
11 Wed 9:59 am	Virgo	Earth	Barren	2nd
12 Thu	Virgo	Earth	Barren	2nd
13 Fri 11:56 am	Libra	Air	Semi-fruitful	2nd
14 Sat	Libra	Air	Semi-fruitful	2nd
15 Sun 12:31 pm	Scorpio	Water	Fruitful	2nd
16 Mon	Scorpio	Water	Fruitful	2nd
17 Tue 1:22 pm	Sagittarius	Fire	Barren	Full 7:09 am
18 Wed	Sagittarius	Fire	Barren	3rd
19 Thu 4:16 pm	Capricorn	Earth	Semi-fruitful	3rd
20 Fri	Capricorn	Earth	Semi-fruitful	3rd
21 Sat 10:32 pm	Aquarius	Air	Barren	3rd
22 Sun	Aquarius	Air	Barren	3rd
23 Mon	Aquarius	Air	Barren	3rd
24 Tue 8:24 am	Pisces	Water	Fruitful	4th 2:52 pm
25 Wed	Pisces	Water	Fruitful	4th
26 Thu 8:36 pm	Aries	Fire	Barren	4th
27 Fri	Aries	Fire	Barren	4th
28 Sat	Aries	Fire	Barren	4th
29 Sun 9:02 am	Taurus	Earth	Semi-fruitful	4th
30 Mon	Taurus	Earth	Semi-fruitful	4th
31 Tue 7:56 pm	Gemini	Air	Barren	4th

June Moon Table

Date	Sign	Element	Nature	Phase
1 Wed	Gemini	Air	Barren	New 5:03 pm
2 Thu	Gemini	Air	Barren	1st
3 Fri 4:36 am	Cancer	Water	Fruitful	1st
4 Sat	Cancer	Water	Fruitful	1st
5 Sun 11:03 am	Leo	Fire	Barren	1st
6 Mon	Leo	Fire	Barren	1st
7 Tue 3:33 pm	Virgo	Earth	Barren	1st
8 Wed	Virgo	Earth	Barren	2nd 10:11 pm
9 Thu 6:31 pm	Libra	Air	Semi-fruitful	2nd
10 Fri	Libra	Air	Semi-fruitful	2nd
11 Sat 8:33 pm	Scorpio	Water	Fruitful	2nd
12 Sun	Scorpio	Water	Fruitful	2nd
13 Mon 10:38 pm	Sagittarius	Fire	Barren	2nd
14 Tue	Sagittarius	Fire	Barren	2nd
15 Wed	Sagittarius	Fire	Barren	Full 4:14 pm
16 Thu 1:59 am	Capricorn	Earth	Semi-fruitful	3rd
17 Fri	Capricorn	Earth	Semi-fruitful	3rd
18 Sat 7:47 am	Aquarius	Air	Barren	3rd
19 Sun	Aquarius	Air	Barren	3rd
20 Mon 4:45 pm	Pisces	Water	Fruitful	3rd
21 Tue	Pisces	Water	Fruitful	3rd
22 Wed	Pisces	Water	Fruitful	3rd
23 Thu 4:24 am	Aries	Fire	Barren	4th 7:48 am
24 Fri	Aries	Fire	Barren	4th
25 Sat 4:53 pm	Taurus	Earth	Semi-fruitful	4th
26 Sun	Taurus	Earth	Semi-fruitful	4th
27 Mon	Taurus	Earth	Semi-fruitful	4th
28 Tue 3:56 am	Gemini	Air	Barren	4th
29 Wed	Gemini	Air	Barren	4th
30 Thu 12:13 pm	Cancer	Water	Fruitful	4th

July Moon Table

Date	Sign	Element	Nature	Phase
1 Fri	Cancer	Water	Fruitful	New 4:54 am
2 Sat 5:43 pm	Leo	Fire	Barren	1st
3 Sun	Leo	Fire	Barren	1st
4 Mon 9:15 pm	Virgo	Earth	Barren	1st
5 Tue	Virgo	Earth	Barren	1st
6 Wed 11:54 pm	Libra	Air	Semi-fruitful	1st
7 Thu	Libra	Air	Semi-fruitful	1st
8 Fri	Libra	Air	Semi-fruitful	2nd 2:29 am
9 Sat 2:31 am	Scorpio	Water	Fruitful	2nd
10 Sun	Scorpio	Water	Fruitful	2nd
11 Mon 5:47 am	Sagittarius	Fire	Barren	2nd
12 Tue	Sagittarius	Fire	Barren	2nd
13 Wed 10:14 am	Capricorn	Earth	Semi-fruitful	2nd
14 Thu	Capricorn	Earth	Semi-fruitful	2nd
15 Fri 4:30 pm	Aquarius	Air	Barren	Full 2:40 am
16 Sat	Aquarius	Air	Barren	3rd
17 Sun	Aquarius	Air	Barren	3rd
18 Mon 1:13 am	Pisces	Water	Fruitful	3rd
19 Tue	Pisces	Water	Fruitful	3rd
20 Wed 12:25 pm	Aries	Fire	Barren	3rd
21 Thu	Aries	Fire	Barren	3rd
22 Fri	Aries	Fire	Barren	3rd
23 Sat 12:58 am	Taurus	Earth	Semi-fruitful	4th 1:02 am
24 Sun	Taurus	Earth	Semi-fruitful	4th
25 Mon 12:34 pm	Gemini	Air	Barren	4th
26 Tue	Gemini	Air	Barren	4th
27 Wed 9:11 pm	Cancer	Water	Fruitful	4th
28 Thu	Cancer	Water	Fruitful	4th
29 Fri	Cancer	Water	Fruitful	4th
30 Sat 2:16 am	Leo	Fire	Barren	New 2:40 pm
31 Sun	Leo	Fire	Barren	1st

August Moon Table

Date	Sign	Element	Nature	Phase
1 Mon 4:41 am	Virgo	Earth	Barren	1st
2 Tue	Virgo	Earth	Barren	1st
3 Wed 6:04 am	Libra	Air	Semi-fruitful	1st
4 Thu	Libra	Air	Semi-fruitful	1st
5 Fri 7:57 am	Scorpio	Water	Fruitful	1st
6 Sat	Scorpio	Water	Fruitful	2nd 7:08 am
7 Sun 11:21 am	Sagittarius	Fire	Barren	2nd
8 Mon	Sagittarius	Fire	Barren	2nd
9 Tue 4:38 pm	Capricorn	Earth	Semi-fruitful	2nd
10 Wed	Capricorn	Earth	Semi-fruitful	2nd
11 Thu 11:47 pm	Aquarius	Air	Barren	2nd
12 Fri	Aquarius	Air	Barren	2nd
13 Sat	Aquarius	Air	Barren	Full 2:58 pm
14 Sun 8:54 am	Pisces	Water	Fruitful	3rd
15 Mon	Pisces	Water	Fruitful	3rd
16 Tue 8:01 pm	Aries	Fire	Barren	3rd
17 Wed	Aries	Fire	Barren	3rd
18 Thu	Aries	Fire	Barren	3rd
19 Fri 8:36 am	Taurus	Earth	Semi-fruitful	3rd
20 Sat	Taurus	Earth	Semi-fruitful	3rd
21 Sun 8:53 pm	Gemini	Air	Barren	4th 5:54 pm
22 Mon	Gemini	Air	Barren	4th
23 Tue	Gemini	Air	Barren	4th
24 Wed 6:31 am	Cancer	Water	Fruitful	4th
25 Thu	Cancer	Water	Fruitful	4th
26 Fri 12:09 pm	Leo	Fire	Barren	4th
27 Sat	Leo	Fire	Barren	4th
28 Sun 2:13 pm	Virgo	Earth	Barren	New 11:04 pm
29 Mon	Virgo	Earth	Barren	1st
30 Tue 2:25 pm	Libra	Air	Semi-fruitful	1st
31 Wed	Libra	Air	Semi-fruitful	1st

September Moon Table

Date	Sign	Element	Nature	Phase
1 Thu 2:48 pm	Scorpio	Water	Fruitful	1st
2 Fri	Scorpio	Water	Fruitful	1st
3 Sat 5:03 pm	Sagittarius	Fire	Barren	1st
4 Sun	Sagittarius	Fire	Barren	2nd 1:39 pm
5 Mon 10:03 pm	Capricorn	Earth	Semi-fruitful	2nd
6 Tue	Capricorn	Earth	Semi-fruitful	2nd
7 Wed	Capricorn	Earth	Semi-fruitful	2nd
8 Thu 5:42 am	Aquarius	Air	Barren	2nd
9 Fri	Aquarius	Air	Barren	2nd
10 Sat 3:26 pm	Pisces	Water	Fruitful	2nd
11 Sun	Pisces	Water	Fruitful	2nd
12 Mon	Pisces	Water	Fruitful	Full 5:27 am
13 Tue 2:49 am	Aries	Fire	Barren	3rd
14 Wed	Aries	Fire	Barren	3rd
15 Thu 3:25 pm	Taurus	Earth	Semi-fruitful	3rd
16 Fri	Taurus	Earth	Semi-fruitful	3rd
17 Sat	Taurus	Earth	Semi-fruitful	3rd
18 Sun 4:06 am	Gemini	Air	Barren	3rd
19 Mon	Gemini	Air	Barren	3rd
20 Tue 2:53 pm	Cancer	Water	Fruitful	4th 9:39 am
21 Wed	Cancer	Water	Fruitful	4th
22 Thu 9:55 pm	Leo	Fire	Barren	4th
23 Fri	Leo	Fire	Barren	4th
24 Sat	Leo	Fire	Barren	4th
25 Sun 12:49 am	Virgo	Earth	Barren	4th
26 Mon	Virgo	Earth	Barren	4th
27 Tue 12:51 am	Libra	Air	Semi-fruitful	New 7:09 am
28 Wed	Libra	Air	Semi-fruitful	1st
29 Thu 12:05 am	Scorpio	Water	Fruitful	1st
30 Fri	Scorpio	Water	Fruitful	1st

October Moon Table

Date	Sign	Element	Nature	Phase
1 Sat 12:42 am	Sagittarius	Fire	Barren	1st
2 Sun	Sagittarius	Fire	Barren	1st
3 Mon 4:16 am	Capricorn	Earth	Semi-fruitful	2nd 11:15 pm
4 Tue	Capricorn	Earth	Semi-fruitful	2nd
5 Wed 11:18 am	Aquarius	Air	Barren	2nd
6 Thu	Aquarius	Air	Barren	2nd
7 Fri 9:13 pm	Pisces	Water	Fruitful	2nd
8 Sat	Pisces	Water	Fruitful	2nd
9 Sun	Pisces	Water	Fruitful	2nd
10 Mon 8:57 am	Aries	Fire	Barren	2nd
11 Tue	Aries	Fire	Barren	Full 10:06 pm
12 Wed 9:35 pm	Taurus	Earth	Semi-fruitful	3rd
13 Thu	Taurus	Earth	Semi-fruitful	3rd
14 Fri	Taurus	Earth	Semi-fruitful	3rd
15 Sat 10:15 am	Gemini	Air	Barren	3rd
16 Sun	Gemini	Air	Barren	3rd
17 Mon 9:38 pm	Cancer	Water	Fruitful	3rd
18 Tue	Cancer	Water	Fruitful	3rd
19 Wed	Cancer	Water	Fruitful	4th 11:30 pm
20 Thu 6:06 am	Leo	Fire	Barren	4th
21 Fri	Leo	Fire	Barren	4th
22 Sat 10:40 am	Virgo	Earth	Barren	4th
23 Sun	Virgo	Earth	Barren	4th
24 Mon 11:49 am	Libra	Air	Semi-fruitful	4th
25 Tue	Libra	Air	Semi-fruitful	4th
26 Wed 11:08 am	Scorpio	Water	Fruitful	New 3:56 pm
27 Thu	Scorpio	Water	Fruitful	1st
28 Fri 10:45 am	Sagittarius	Fire	Barren	1st
29 Sat	Sagittarius	Fire	Barren	1st
30 Sun 12:39 pm	Capricorn	Earth	Semi-fruitful	1st
31 Mon	Capricorn	Earth	Semi-fruitful	1st

November Moon Table

Date	Sign	Element	Nature	Phase
1 Tue 6:08 pm	Aquarius	Air	Barren	1st
2 Wed	Aquarius	Air	Barren	2nd 12:38 pm
3 Thu	Aquarius	Air	Barren	2nd
4 Fri 3:18 am	Pisces	Water	Fruitful	2nd
5 Sat	Pisces	Water	Fruitful	2nd
6 Sun 2:02 pm	Aries	Fire	Barren	2nd
7 Mon	Aries	Fire	Barren	2nd
8 Tue	Aries	Fire	Barren	2nd
9 Wed 2:45 am	Taurus	Earth	Semi-fruitful	2nd
10 Thu	Taurus	Earth	Semi-fruitful	Full 3:16 pm
11 Fri 3:10 pm	Gemini	Air	Barren	3rd
12 Sat	Gemini	Air	Barren	3rd
13 Sun	Gemini	Air	Barren	3rd
14 Mon 2:19 am	Cancer	Water	Fruitful	3rd
15 Tue	Cancer	Water	Fruitful	3rd
16 Wed 11:17 am	Leo	Fire	Barren	3rd
17 Thu	Leo	Fire	Barren	3rd
18 Fri 5:19 pm	Virgo	Earth	Barren	4th 10:09 am
19 Sat	Virgo	Earth	Barren	4th
20 Sun 8:16 pm	Libra	Air	Semi-fruitful	4th
21 Mon	Libra	Air	Semi-fruitful	4th
22 Tue 8:58 pm	Scorpio	Water	Fruitful	4th
23 Wed	Scorpio	Water	Fruitful	4th
24 Thu 8:57 pm	Sagittarius	Fire	Barren	4th
25 Fri	Sagittarius	Fire	Barren	New 1:10 am
26 Sat 10:05 pm	Capricorn	Earth	Semi-fruitful	1st
27 Sun	Capricorn	Earth	Semi-fruitful	1st
28 Mon	Capricorn	Earth	Semi-fruitful	1st
29 Tue 2:02 am	Aquarius	Air	Barren	1st
30 Wed	Aquarius	Air	Barren	1st

December Moon Table

Date	Sign	Element	Nature	Phase
1 Thu 9:45 am	Pisces	Water	Fruitful	1st
2 Fri	Pisces	Water	Fruitful	2nd 4:52 am
3 Sat 8:51 pm	Aries	Fire	Barren	2nd
4 Sun	Aries	Fire	Barren	2nd
5 Mon	Aries	Fire	Barren	2nd
6 Tue 9:34 am	Taurus	Earth	Semi-fruitful	2nd
7 Wed	Taurus	Earth	Semi-fruitful	2nd
8 Thu 9:52 pm	Gemini	Air	Barren	2nd
9 Fri	Gemini	Air	Barren	2nd
10 Sat	Gemini	Air	Barren	Full 9:36 am
11 Sun 8:26 am	Cancer	Water	Fruitful	3rd
12 Mon	Cancer	Water	Fruitful	3rd
13 Tue 4:48 pm	Leo	Fire	Barren	3rd
14 Wed	Leo	Fire	Barren	3rd
15 Thu 10:58 pm	Virgo	Earth	Barren	3rd
16 Fri	Virgo	Earth	Barren	3rd
17 Sat	Virgo	Earth	Barren	4th 7:48 pm
18 Sun 3:06 am	Libra	Air	Semi-fruitful	4th
19 Mon	Libra	Air	Semi-fruitful	4th
20 Tue 5:33 am	Scorpio	Water	Fruitful	4th
21 Wed	Scorpio	Water	Fruitful	4th
22 Thu 7:03 am	Sagittarius	Fire	Barren	4th
23 Fri	Sagittarius	Fire	Barren	4th
24 Sat 8:47 am	Capricorn	Earth	Semi-fruitful	New 1:06 pm
25 Sun	Capricorn	Earth	Semi-fruitful	1st
26 Mon 12:14 pm	Aquarius	Air	Barren	1st
27 Tue	Aquarius	Air	Barren	1st
28 Wed 6:45 pm	Pisces	Water	Fruitful	1st
29 Thu	Pisces	Water	Fruitful	1st
30 Fri	Pisces	Water	Fruitful	1st
31 Sat 4:48 am	Aries	Fire	Barren	1st

Dates to Destroy Weeds and Pests

From		To		Sign	Qtr
Jan 19	5:16 pm	Jan 21	6:10 pm	Leo	3rd
Jan 21	6:10 pm	Jan 23	6:59 pm	Virgo	3rd
Jan 28	1:55 am	Jan 30	9:04 am	Sagittarius	4th
Feb 1	6:21 pm	Feb 2	9:31 pm	Aquarius	4th
Feb 18	3:36 am	Feb 18	4:39 am	Leo	3rd
Feb 18	4:39 am	Feb 20	4:01 am	Virgo	3rd
Feb 24	7:46 am	Feb 24	6:26 pm	Sagittarius	3rd
Feb 24	6:26 pm	Feb 26	2:32 pm	Sagittarius	4th
Mar 1	12:14 am	Mar 3	11:47 am	Aquarius	4th
Mar 19	2:10 pm	Mar 19	4:03 pm	Virgo	3rd
Mar 23	4:45 pm	Mar 25	9:57 pm	Sagittarius	3rd
Mar 28	7:00 am	Mar 30	6:38 pm	Aquarius	4th
Apr 2	7:16 am	Apr 3	10:32 am	Aries	4th
Apr 20	2:50 am	Apr 22	6:24 am	Sagittarius	3rd
Apr 24	1:59 pm	Apr 24	10:47 pm	Aquarius	3rd
Apr 24	10:47 pm	Apr 27	12:57 am	Aquarius	4th
Apr 29	1:33 pm	May 2	1:58 am	Aries	4th
May 17	1:22 pm	May 19	4:16 pm	Sagittarius	3rd
May 21	10:32 pm	May 24	8:24 am	Aquarius	3rd
May 26	8:36 pm	May 29	9:02 am	Aries	4th
May 31	7:56 pm	Jun 1	5:03 pm	Gemini	4th
Jun 15	4:14 pm	Jun 16	1:59 am	Sagittarius	3rd
Jun 18	7:47 am	Jun 20	4:45 pm	Aquarius	3rd
Jun 23	4:24 am	Jun 23	7:48 am	Aries	3rd
Jun 23	7:48 am	Jun 25	4:53 pm	Aries	4th
Jun 28	3:56 am	Jun 30	12:13 pm	Gemini	4th
Jul 15	4:30 pm	Jul 18	1:13 am	Aquarius	3rd
Jul 20	12:25 pm	Jul 23	12:58 am	Aries	3rd
Jul 25	12:34 pm	Jul 27	9:11 pm	Gemini	4th
Jul 30	2:16 am	Jul 30	2:40 pm	Leo	4th
Aug 13	2:58 pm	Aug 14	8:54 am	Aquarius	3rd
Aug 16	8:01 pm	Aug 19	8:36 am	Aries	3rd
Aug 21	8:53 pm	Aug 24	6:31 am	Gemini	4th

From		To		Sign	Qtr
Aug 26	12:09 pm	Aug 28	2:13 pm	Leo	4th
Aug 28	2:13 pm	Aug 28	11:04 pm	Virgo	4th
Sep 13	2:49 am	Sep 15	3:25 pm	Aries	3rd
Sep 18	4:06 am	Sep 20	9:39 am	Gemini	3rd
Sep 20	9:39 am	Sep 20	2:53 pm	Gemini	4th
Sep 22	9:55 pm	Sep 25	12:49 am	Leo	4th
Sep 25	12:49 am	Sep 27	12:51 am	Virgo	4th
Oct 11	10:06 pm	Oct 12	9:35 pm	Aries	3rd
Oct 15	10:15 am	Oct 17	9:38 pm	Gemini	3rd
Oct 20	6:06 am	Oct 22	10:40 am	Leo	4th
Oct 22	10:40 am	Oct 24	11:49 am	Virgo	4th
Nov 11	3:10 pm	Nov 14	2:19 am	Gemini	3rd
Nov 16	11:17 am	Nov 18	10:09 am	Leo	3rd
Nov 18	10:09 am	Nov 18	5:19 pm	Leo	4th
Nov 18	5:19 pm	Nov 20	8:16 pm	Virgo	4th
Nov 24	8:57 pm	Nov 25	1:10 am	Sagittarius	4th
Dec 10	9:36 am	Dec 11	8:26 am	Gemini	3rd
Dec 13	4:48 pm	Dec 15	10:58 pm	Leo	3rd
Dec 15	10:58 pm	Dec 17	7:48 pm	Virgo	3rd
Dec 17	7:48 pm	Dec 18	3:06 am	Virgo	4th
Dec 22	7:03 am	Dec 24	8:47 am	Sagittarius	4th

About the Authors

ELIZABETH BARRETTE serves as the managing editor of *Pan-Gaia*. The central Illinois resident has been involved with the Pagan community for more than seventeen years. Her other writing fields include speculative fiction and gender studies. Visit her Web site at www.worthlink.net/~ysabet/sitemap.html.

CHANDRA MOIRA BEAL is a freelance writer currently living in England. She has authored three books and published hundreds of articles, all inspired by her day-to-day life and adventures. She has been writing for Llewellyn since 1998. Chandra is also a massage therapist. To learn more, visit www.beal-net.com/laluna.

NANCY V. BENNETT has been published in Llewellyn's annuals, *We'moon*, *Circle Network*, and many mainstream publications. Her pet projects include reading and writing about history and creating ethnic dinners to test on her family.

CALANTIRNIEL has worked with herbs and natural healing since the early 1990s and became a certified Master Herbalist in 2007. She lives in western Montana with her husband and daughter while her son is off to college. She also manages to have an organic garden and crochets professionally. Find out more at www.myspace.com/aartiana.

DALLAS JENNIFER COBB lives in an enchanted waterfront village where she focuses on what she loves: family, gardens, fitness, and fabulous food. Her essays are in Llewellyn's almanacs and recent Seal Press anthologies *Three Ring Circus* and

Far From Home. Her video documentary, *Disparate Places*, appeared on TV Ontario's *Planet Parent*. Contact her at Jennifer. Cobb@Sympatico.ca.

SALLY CRAGIN writes the astrological forecast, "Moon Signs," for the *Boston Phoenix*, which is syndicated throughout New England. She can also be heard on several radio stations as "Symboline Dai." A regular arts reviewer and feature writer for the *Boston Globe*, she also edits *Button, New England's Tiniest Magazine of Poetry, Fiction, and Gracious Living*. For more, including your personal forecast that clients have called "scary-accurate," see http://moonsigns.net.

ALICE DEVILLE is an internationally known astrologer, writer, and metaphysical consultant. She has been both a reiki and seichim master since 1996. In her northern Virginia practice, Alice specializes in relationships, health, healing, real estate, government affairs, career and change management, and spiritual development. Contact Alice at DeVilleAA@aol.com.

ELLEN EVERT HOPMAN is a master herbalist, and the author of books on Celtic herb lore and Celtic ritual uses of plants. She teaches herbalism in workshops throughout the United States and in Europe. Visit her Web site at http://www .EllenEvertHopman.com.

JD HORTWORT resides in North Carolina. She is an avid student of herbology and gardening, a professional writer, and an award-winning journalist.

MISTY KUCERIS has worked as a plant specialist during the last several years for various nurseries in the Greater DC metropolitan area. As a plant consultant, she meets with homeowners to assess their property and gardens. She also lectures at garden clubs and senior citizen centers giving guidance and advice on how to create healthy home gardens and lawns. At the time of this printing, Misty's gardening Web site is under construction. You can contact her at Misty@EnhanceOneself.com with any questions.

SUSAN PESZNECKER is a hearth pagan and a child of the natural world in all of its magickal guises. Areas of expertise include astronomy, herbology, healing, stonework, nature study, and folklore. As a fourth-generation Oregonian, Susan is an aficionado of the rock art of Northwest Coastal and Columbia Plateau First People. She loves to read, camp, and work in her organic garden. She makes her home in Milwaukie, Oregon.

SUZANNE RESS has been writing fiction and nonfiction for an eclectic array of publications for more than twenty-five years. She is an accomplished self-taught gardener and silversmith/mosiacist. She lives in the woods at the foot of the Alps in northern Italy with her husband, two teenage daughters, wolf dog, and two horses.

LAUREL REUFNER lives in gorgeous Athens County, Ohio, with her husband and two daughters. Attracted to topics of history and mythology, she is working on her first book. Keep up with her at her blog Tryl's Meanderings at trylsmeanderings .blogspot.com.

ANNE SALA currently, she lives and works as a freelance journalist in Minnesota, where she hunts wild asparagus.

CAROLE SCHWALM lives in Sante Fe, New Mexico. She has contributed to self-help articles and writes for America Online and other Web sites.

HARMONY USHER lives in Prince Edward County, Ontario, with her two children, a super dog, and a magical boy rabbit.

KATHERINE WEBER-TURCOTTE Is an herbalist, avid gardener and Green Witch living in the Pine Barrens of New Jersey. She is also a student of Clayton College of Natural Health. Look for her articles in *Herb Quarterly* magazine where she is a regular contributor. You can read her blogs at: http://www.enchantedwoodmusings.blogspot.com and http://www.grit.com/blogs/blog.aspx?blogid=3264, or contact her by e-mail at: kathy@enchantedwoodherbs.com

~Notes~

~Notes~

~Notes~